The **Essential** Buyer's Guide

LOTUS
ELAN

S1 to Sprint and Plus 2 to Plus 2S 130/5
1962 to 1974

Your marque expert:
Matthew Vale

VELOCE PUBLISHING
THE PUBLISHER OF FINE AUTOMOTIVE BOOKS

Essential Buyer's Guide Series

Alfa Romeo Alfasud (Metcalfe)
Alfa Romeo Alfetta: all saloon/sedan models 1972 to 1984 & coupé models 1974 to 1987 (Metcalfe)
Alfa Romeo Giulia GT Coupé (Booker)
Alfa Romeo Giulia Spider (Booker)
Audi TT (Davies)
Audi TT Mk2 2006 to 2014 (Durnan)
Austin-Healey Big Healeys (Trummel)
BMW Boxer Twins (Henshaw)
BMW E30 3 Series 1981 to 1994 (Hosier)
BMW GS (Henshaw)
BMW X5 (Saunders)
BMW Z3 Roadster (Fishwick)
BMW Z4: E85 Roadster and E86 Coupe including M and Alpina 2003 to 2009 (Smitheram)
BSA 350, 441 & 500 Singles (Henshaw)
BSA 500 & 650 Twins (Henshaw)
BSA Bantam (Henshaw)
Choosing, Using & Maintaining Your Electric Bicycle (Henshaw)
Citroën 2CV (Paxton)
Citroën ID & DS (Heilig)
Cobra Replicas (Ayre)
Corvette C2 Sting Ray 1963-1967 (Falconer)
Datsun 240Z 1969 to 1973 (Newlyn)
DeLorean DMC-12 1981 to 1983 (Williams)
Ducati Bevel Twins (Falloon)
Ducati Desmodue Twins (Falloon)
Ducati Desmoquattro Twins – 851, 888, 916, 996, 998, ST4, 1988 to 2004 (Falloon)
Fiat 500 & 600 (Bobbitt)
Ford Capri (Paxton)
Ford Escort Mk1 & Mk2 (Williamson)
Ford Model A – All Models 1927 to 1931 (Buckley)
Ford Model T – All models 1909 to 1927 (Barker)
Ford Mustang – First Generation 1964 to 1973 (Cook)
Ford Mustang (Cook)
Ford RS Cosworth Sierra & Escort (Williamson)
Harley-Davidson Big Twins (Henshaw)
Hillman Imp (Morgan)
Hinckley Triumph triples & fours 750, 900, 955, 1000, 1050, 1200 – 1991-2009 (Henshaw)
Honda CBR FireBlade (Henshaw)
Honda CBR600 Hurricane (Henshaw)
Honda SOHC Fours 1969-1984 (Henshaw)
Jaguar E-Type 3.8 & 4.2 litre (Crespin)
Jaguar E-type V12 5.3 litre (Crespin)
Jaguar Mark 1 & 2 (All models including Daimler 2.5-litre V8) 1955 to 1969 (Thorley)
Jaguar New XK 2005-2014 (Thorley)
Jaguar S-Type – 1999 to 2007 (Thorley)
Jaguar X-Type – 2001 to 2009 (Thorley)
Jaguar XJ-S (Crespin)
Jaguar XJ6, XJ8 & XJR (Thorley)
Jaguar XK 120, 140 & 150 (Thorley)
Jaguar XK8 & XKR (1996-2005) (Thorley)
Jaguar/Daimler XJ 1994-2003 (Crespin)
Jaguar/Daimler XJ40 (Crespin)
Jaguar/Daimler XJ6, XJ12 & Sovereign (Crespin)
Kawasaki Z1 & Z900 (Orritt)
Land Rover Discovery Series 1 (1989-1998) (Taylor)
Land Rover Discovery Series 2 (1998-2004) (Taylor)
Land Rover Series I, II & IIA (Thurman)
Land Rover Series III (Thurman)
Lotus Elan (Vale)
Lotus Europa (Vale)
Lotus Seven replicas & Caterham 7: 1973-2013 (Hawkins)
Mazda MX-5 Miata (Mk1 1989-97 & Mk2 98-2001) (Crook)
Mazda RX-8 (Parish)
Mercedes Benz Pagoda 230SL, 250SL & 280SL roadsters & coupés (Bass)
Mercedes-Benz 190: all 190 models (W201 series) 1982 to 1993 (Parish)
Mercedes-Benz 280-560SL & SLC (Bass)
Mercedes-Benz SL R129-series 1989 to 2001 (Parish)
Mercedes-Benz SLK (Bass)
Mercedes-Benz W123 (Parish)
Mercedes-Benz W124 – All models 1984-1997 (Zoporowski)
MG Midget & A-H Sprite (Horler)
MG TD, TF & TF1500 (Jones)
MGA 1955-1962 (Crosier)
MGB & MGB GT (Williams)
MGF & MG TF (Hawkins)
Mini (Paxton)
Morris Minor & 1000 (Newell)
Moto Guzzi 2-valve big twins (Falloon)
New Mini (Collins)
Norton Commando (Henshaw)
Peugeot 205 GTI (Blackburn)
Piaggio Scooters – all modern two-stroke & four-stroke automatic models 1991 to 2016 (Willis)
Porsche 911 (964) (Streather)
Porsche 911 (993) (Streather)
Porsche 911 (996) (Streather)
Porsche 911 (997) – Model years 2004 to 2009 (Streather)
Porsche 911 (997) – Second generation models 2009 to 2012 (Streather)
Porsche 911 Carrera 3.2 (Streather)
Porsche 911SC (Streather)
Porsche 924 – All models 1976 to 1988 (Hodgkins)
Porsche 928 (Hemmings)
Porsche 930 Turbo & 911 (930) Turbo (Streather)
Porsche 944 (Higgins)
Porsche 981 Boxster & Cayman (Streather)
Porsche 986 Boxster (Streather)
Porsche 987 Boxster and Cayman 1st generation (2005-2009) (Streather)
Porsche 987 Boxster and Cayman 2nd generation (2009-2012) (Streather)
Range Rover – First Generation models 1970 to 1996 (Taylor)
Rolls-Royce Silver Shadow & Bentley T-Series (Bobbitt)
Royal Enfield Bullet (Henshaw)
Subaru Impreza (Hobbs)
Sunbeam Alpine (Barker)
Triumph 350 & 500 Twins (Henshaw)
Triumph Bonneville (Henshaw)
Triumph Stag (Mort)
Triumph Thunderbird, Trophy & Tiger (Henshaw)
Triumph TR6 (Williams)
Triumph TR7 & TR8 (Williams)
Velocette 350 & 500 Singles 1946 to 1970 (Henshaw)
Vespa Scooters – Classic two-stroke models 1960-2008 (Paxton)
Volkswagen Bus (Copping)
Volvo 700/900 Series (Beavis)
Volvo P1800/1800S, E & ES 1961 to 1973 (Murray)
VW Beetle (Copping)
VW Golf GTI (Copping)

www.veloce.co.uk

First published in October 2018 by Veloce Publishing Limited, Veloce House, Parkway Farm Business Park, Middle Farm Way, Poundbury, Dorchester DT1 3AR, England. Tel +44 (0)1305 260068 / Fax 01305 250479 / e-mail info@veloce.co.uk / web www.veloce.co.uk or www.velocebooks.com.
ISBN: 978-1-787112-86-5 UPC: 6-36847-01286-1. © 2018 Matthew Vale and Veloce Publishing. All rights reserved. With the exception of quoting brief passages for the purpose of review, no part of this publication may be recorded, reproduced or transmitted by any means, including photocopying, without the written permission of Veloce Publishing Ltd. Throughout this book logos, model names and designations, etc, have been used for the purposes of identification, illustration and decoration. Such names are the property of the trademark holder as this is not an official publication. Readers with ideas for automotive books, or books on other transport or related hobby subjects, are invited to write to the editorial director of Veloce Publishing at the above address. British Library Cataloguing in Publication Data – A catalogue record for this book is available from the British Library. Typesetting, design and page make-up all by Veloce Publishing Ltd on Apple Mac. Printed in India by Replika Press.

Introduction
– the purpose of this book

The Lotus Elan and its larger brother, the Plus 2, were the antithesis of the hairy-chested British sports car. Lightweight, delicate and finely engineered, the cars rewarded sensitive drivers with outstanding levels of handling and roadholding, and class-leading performance. Both the Elan and Plus 2 were outstanding small sports cars, which made Lotus' reputation as a maker of fast road cars. They were also relatively affordable, when compared with Lotus' previous road car, the Type 14 Elite.

Designed by a small team of talented engineers, headed by Ron Hickman and overseen by Lotus founder Colin Chapman, the Lotus Elan was constructed by placing a glass fibre bodyshell on a backbone chassis made from lightweight pressed steel sheet. This format would become the standard configuration for Lotus road cars of the '60s, through to the '90s. Initially, the convertible Elan was offered to the home market in right-hand drive form, but was quickly built in left-hand drive format, and distributed to the European and American markets. Powered by Lotus' own engine, the Twin-Cam, the Elan had around 105bhp, and its light weight gave it sparkling performance.

A racing version, the Lotus 26R, was introduced alongside the Series 1 in 1964, and had a lightly modified and strengthened chassis, as well as various mechanical upgrades and a tuned Twin-Cam engine. This is a specialist vehicle, and is outside the scope of this book.

The Series 2 Elan, introduced in 1967, had a number of improvements over the Series 1. Around that time the SE version was launched, which had some cosmetic improvements and a 115bhp engine.

This is a fine example of the first of the line – a Series 1 Lotus Elan. With the top down the car epitomises the small British sports car.

The next version of the Elan was the Coupé. With its fixed roof, the Coupé offered the Elan driver more creature comforts.

The last iteration of the Elan was the Sprint. With a highly tuned twin-cam engine, the car was the ultimate performance Elan.

The Elan Coupé appeared in 1965, giving the customer the choice of a closed coupé. The Series 3 was introduced in 1966 in drophead and fixed-head forms, and featured a revised bodyshell and slightly more upmarket interior, along with a better hood and electric windows.

The Series 4 came out in 1968, with slightly flared wheelarches allowing for the fitment of wider tyres. The final version, the Sprint, appeared in 1971. Fitted with the 'Big Valve' version of the Twin-Cam, which produced 126bhp, the Sprint was the fastest of all the Elans. A few were fitted with a Lotus five-speed gearbox, right at the end of production in 1973.

The Plus 2 was, as its name suggests, a 2+2 with a pair of small rear seats. With a lengthened and widened chassis, the Plus 2 shared its mechanical underpinnings with the original Elan.

A widened and lengthened version, the Plus 2, appeared in 1967. It had limited rear seating and a more upmarket image. Equipped with the SE specification engine, the Plus 2 was a high-performance GT car with the capacity to seat two children in the back. The Plus 2S was introduced in 1969 as a more upmarket version of the Plus 2, with a higher specification for the interior, and the Plus 2S 130, introduced in 1971, was fitted with the big valve Sprint engine to give a boost to performance. In 1972, the Plus 2 was given a five-speed gearbox option, creating the Plus 2S 130/5. Plus 2 production finally finished at the end of 1974.

The Elan and Plus 2 are delicate and potentially fragile cars, built with Chapman's adage of 'add lightness' firmly in mind. While a good Elan or Plus 2 is a delight to drive and own, finding one is not so easy. While the cars are past the 'banger' stage, when buying you must be careful. You need to understand that the Elan is not just another sports car, but a finely crafted, carefully engineered classic which does not respond well to rough treatment by careless owners or mechanics. This book will help prospective owners understand the subtleties of Elan and Plus 2 ownership, and will help to guide them towards finding a great example.

The Elan and Plus 2 are closely related. In this shot, the extra width of the Plus 2 is apparent.

Contents

Introduction
– the purpose of this book 3

1 Is it the right car for you?
– marriage guidance 6

2 Cost considerations
– affordable, or a money pit? 10

3 Living with an Elan
– will you get along together? 12

4 Relative values
– which model for you? 14

5 Before you view
– be well informed 20

6 Inspection equipment
– these items will really help 23

7 Fifteen minute evaluation
– walk away or stay? 24

8 Key points
– where to look for problems 27

9 Serious evaluation
– 60 minutes for years of enjoyment .. 29

10 Auctions
– sold! Another way to buy your dream 45

11 Paperwork
– correct documentation is essential! 47

12 What's it worth?
– let your head rule your heart 49

13 Do you really want to restore?
– it'll take longer and cost more than you think 51

14 Paint problems
– bad complexion, including dimples, pimples and bubbles 53

15 Problems due to lack of use
– just like their owners, Elans need exercise! 55

16 The Community
– key people, organisations and companies in the Elan world 56

17 Vital statistics
– essential data at your fingertips 58

Index 64

The Essential Buyer's Guide™ currency
At the time of publication a BG unit of currency "●" equals approximately £1.00/US$1.34/Euro 1.14. Please adjust to suit current exchange rates using Sterling as the base currency.

1 Is it the right car for you?
– marriage guidance

Is the car comfortable?

The Elan and Plus 2 are cars which share their basic mechanical elements, but provide two very different ownership experiences. The Elan is a small, spartan two-seat sports car, with the option of an open top. The Plus 2 is a stretched and widened Elan, with a pair of child-sized rear seats and a fixed roof, which makes it a more sophisticated and luxurious grand tourer. While the Elan is quite small, it has a nicely trimmed cockpit, which includes a wooden dashboard and a full complement of instruments. Its long and wide opening doors facilitate ingress and egress, especially when the hood is down. Access is still good with the hood up, or in the coupé. Once seated, there is plenty of room for the driver and passenger. The Series 1 and Series 2 soft tops are crude 'build-it-yourself' affairs, and take some time to put up and down. The complete hood needs to be dismantled, taken off the car and stowed, either behind the seats or in the boot – a simple but time-consuming process.

The Series 3, 4 and Sprint hoods have a much more convenient folding design, with a hinged frame bolted to the body and the hood attached to the frame. When furled, the later hood sits neatly in a well behind the seats, and is much easier to erect than the previous version. From 1965, a closed coupé version of the Elan was offered alongside the open-topped version.

The Plus 2 was only available from the factory as a two-door coupé, and offered more interior space than the

Series 1 Elans had half-width dashboards and sparsely furnished interiors, with more attention directed at driving pleasure.

The Plus 2 was much more luxurious than the early Elan. This Plus 2 cabin shows the full-width walnut-veneered dash, with its comprehensive complement of gauges and switches.

The rear seats of the Plus 2 are small and not particularly well padded. They are really only suitable for small children.

Elan. It had a luxuriously appointed cockpit, with a veneered wooden dash, lots of minor instruments and well-padded, fully adjustable seats. The Plus 2's doors also open wide and, like the Elan, the front edge of the door is extended ahead of the windscreen, so access is good. The rear seats are strictly for children only, but they add a certain utility to the design. The fixtures and fittings of the interior are a cut above that of the Elan.

Driving

Both the Elan and the Plus 2 benefit from Chapman's design genius, but they're still 1960s sports cars, and while the suspension gives long travel with soft springing and well-controlled damping, the ride is not limousine-smooth. The steering is sharp and direct; the engine is positioned relatively close to the occupants, and there is little soundproofing as standard, so it can be heard and felt. On the road, the Elan and the Plus 2 are joys to drive, giving an involving and engaging experience that is miles away from an anodyne modern hatchback. The Elan is a fast, quick-witted sports car with a well-controlled ride and brilliant handling. The Plus 2, due to its longer wheelbase and wider track, handles even better than the Elan, and gives a more 'mature' ride, with a relaxed feel in line with its 'GT' character. Both cars were designed to be driven fast, and the ride and handling of both add to the great overall owner experience.

Luggage capacity

The Elan has reasonable luggage capacity, both in the boot and inside the cabin behind the seats. The Plus 2 has a larger boot and more cabin space, with plenty of room behind the seats with just two occupants.

Home maintenance

Despite being sports and GT cars with bespoke and sophisticated twin overhead camshaft engines, the Elan and the Plus 2 are fairly easy to maintain at home. The front suspension is Triumph Herald-derived and, while the lower trunnions need regular oiling or greasing, the rest is pretty reliable and easy to access. The rear suspension is all Lotus and fairly simple to maintain. The standard driveshaft 'Rotoflex' rubber donut universal joints need regular inspection, as do the relatively common aftermarket solid driveshafts, which use CV joints or universal joints. The rest just require regular inspection and replacement of bushes and wheel bearings when they wear. Access to the

The Elan has a reasonably-sized boot, perfectly adequate for a weekend's baggage for two or the week's shopping.

All standard Elans were fitted with the Lotus Twin-Cam engine in various states of tune. This Plus 2 engine bay is beautifully presented, and the engine is fitted with Dellorto carburettors.

Lotus Twin-Cam engine is pretty good, although the distributor is buried under the carburettors. The main bugbears of the engine are oil leaks and the water pump. The Twin-Cam often leaks from around the cam cover and the breather tower, between the head and block. Early engines with crankshaft rope seals on the rear main bearing are also prone to leaks. The water pump is pretty reliable, but if the bearing or seals go then replacement is usually a head-off job to gain proper access to the front timing chest it's mounted in. There are aftermarket timing chests available which have 'cartridge' type water pumps, which can be removed from the timing case in situ, avoiding any major dismantling.

Will it fit in your garage?
With the Elan measuring 145in (368.3cm) in length and 56in (142.2cm) in width, and the Plus 2 measuring 168.75in (428.6cm) in length and 66.25in (168.2cm) in width, the good news is that either car will fit in all but the smallest of garages.

Plus points
The Elan and the Plus 2 are massively accomplished sports and GT cars, and they can be incredibly rewarding to own. Their roadholding, performance and handling are up to Lotus' usual high standard, and their small size make both cars wieldy and manoeuvrable. With the Lotus Twin-Cam engine fitted, they were a cut above the products of the other small British sports car manufacturers of the time – they all used proprietary engines from the major manufacturers which were a design generation behind the double overhead cam, alloy-headed Twin-Cam engine. The cars are rare, they have bags of style, and the glass fibre body is rust-free.

Minus points
The Elan is a two-seat sports car and space is limited. The Plus 2 has more room, but with minimal rear seat space. Due to their age and glass fibre body shells, they can suffer from obscure and difficult to diagnose electrical problems. As a 1960s design, the car needs regular servicing and sympathetic handling. The chassis can rust and the body and paint is not immune to deterioration. The Lotus Twin-Cam engine can be a bit of an oil leaker.

Alternatives
There are few alternatives to the Elan from the 1960s and '70s. The Lotus (or Caterham) 7 offers more visceral roadholding and handling, but with significantly fewer creature comforts. The mid-engined Lotus Europa has equivalent handling but less performance in Renault-engined form, and with its small interior and very low stance, it offers less practicality. More direct competitors are glass fibre bodied sports cars from the small British companies, such as TVR, Reliant, Marcos and Gilbern. However, it has to be said that out of all the smaller British

A rival to the Elan is Lotus' own Seven: however, the Seven is a lot more basic than even an early Elan.

sports car manufacturers, Lotus was the only one who produced their own engine, which sets them apart as a 'real' manufacturer. The mainstream competitors are the less sophisticated and more rust-prone MG Midget, MGB, MGB GT and Triumph Spitfire, which are usually cheaper but offer less performance and handling, and the Triumph GT6, TR4, TR5 and TR6, which can offer a similar performance but significantly worse handing and roadholding.

The Alfa Romeo Spider and the Fiat Dino Coupé offer equivalent performance

The mid-engined Lotus Europa, seen behind the Elan Sprint, is another alternative to the Elan from the Lotus stable. It was marketed as a GT car, but still had the trademark Lotus performance and roadholding.

and similar levels of sophistication in their mechanical underpinnings, so they're probably the closest competitors. While the Mazda MX5 is widely touted as an Elan replacement, it's too modern and too heavy, and it doesn't really hit the spot, in the author's opinion. Back in the day, the Jaguar E-Type and the Porsche 911 were often presented as rivals to the Plus 2, but prices of good E-Types and 911s have moved them far above the Plus 2's level in the market.

The TVR Grantura is similar in size and layout to the Elan, with a tubular backbone chassis and glass fibre bodyshell. Many were powered by a mundane BMC 'B' series engine and the handling was not up to Lotus' standard.

Back in the '60s, the E-Type Jaguar was slightly more expensive than the Plus 2, and offered similar levels of space and increased performance. Considered to be a rival back in the '60s and '70s, good E-Types are now far more expensive than Plus 2s.

www.velocebooks.com / www.veloce.co.uk
All current books • New book news • Special offers • Gist vouchers

2 Cost considerations
– affordable, or a money pit?

The Lotus-recommended service intervals for the Elan and Plus 2 are frequent, and reflect the delicate nature and 1960s ancestry of the cars. However, regular servicing of the Elan and Plus 2 is straightforward, and well within the ability of a competent home mechanic. While servicing the Ford-based Lotus Twin-Cam engine is also straightforward, setting the valve clearances needs a selection of shims and the removal of the camshafts, which can be done without taking the head off. Changing the timing chain (there's no set period but expect it needing to be

Access to the Twin-Cam engine in the Elan and Plus 2 is reasonable and the unit is straightforward to service.

done around every 50-75,000 miles) or the water pump seals (unless an aftermarket 'cartridge' pump and front cover is fitted) are really a head-off job. If you are contemplating doing one job then it's worth doing the other while the head is off.

Recommended service intervals for the Lotus Twin-Cam versions is every 5000mi/8000km or 3 months for an 'A' type service. A more rigorous 'B' type service is due every 10,000mi/16,000km or 6 months. Emissions-equipped Twin-Cam engines have additional services on the carburettors every 12,000mi/20,000km and every 24,000mi/40,000km. However, with the limited milage classic cars are usually subjected to, a single service once a year should suffice, along with weekly or pre-use fluid level and safety checks.

Prices: mechanical
Engine
Oil filter: ●x7
Thermostat: ●x6
Water pump repair kit: ●x35
Cartridge style water pump and new front cover: ●x230
Timing chain: ●x19.50
Piston set : ●x480
Piston ring set: ●x120
Big end bearing set: ●x41
Main bearing set: ●x67
Camshaft bearing set: ●x100
Valve guides: ●x8
Valves: ●x11
Gasket set: ●x41
Dellorto carb refurb kit: ●x55
Twin-Cam rebuild: ●x5000

Clutch
Clutch master cylinder: ●x40
Clutch master cylinder repair kit: ●x6
Clutch plate: ●x120
Clutch cover: ●x160
Clutch release bearing: ●x20
Brakes
Master cylinder repair kit: ●x7
Master cylinder repair kit (dual circuit): ●x32
Master cylinder: ●x76
Master cylinder (dual circuit): ●x170
Front brake pads: ●x13
Front brake caliper rebuild kit: ●x13
Front braker caliper piston: ●x12.50
Front brake caliper exchange: ●x50
Front brake disc (pair): ●x28
Rear brake pads: ●x19
Rear brake caliper (reconditioned): ●x70

Rear brake disc (pair): ●x40
Handbrake pads: ●x60
Suspension:
Front trunnions: ●x17.50
Front vertical link: ●x87.50
Top ball joint: ●x9.50
Trackrod end: ●x12.50
Front shock absorber (single): ●x115
Rear shock absorber (pair): ●x212
Rotoflex coupling (x1): ●x70
CV driveshaft kit: ●x400
Miscellaneous:
Alternator: ●x60
Alternator belt: ●x5
Radiator (alloy): ●x140
Headlamp vacuum pod: ●x200
Electric headlamp kit: ●x300

Body parts
While Elan and Plus 2 body panels and complete body shells are available, they tend to be made to order, with prices quoted at that time.

Chassis Elan: from ●x1500
Chassis Plus 2: from ●x1600
Headlight: ●x12
Front indicator and side light: ●x114
Rear light series 4 / Plus 2: ●x195
Rear light lens series 4 / Plus 2: ●x37
Plus 2 sills – stainless steel: ●x229
Plus 2 sills – galvanised: ●x245

Hard-to-find parts
Rear brake calipers are only available as exchange items, and the Carello rear lights fitted to early Plus 2s are very hard to find.

The Elan and Plus 2 backbone chassis is made from folded sheet steel. It's a light and stiff structure but prone to corrosion. Replacement is often a better course than repair.

The Elan Sprint was the last of the line. It was usually supplied in a two-tone finish, as in this blue-over-white example.

3 Living with an Elan
– will you get along together?

The Elan and the Plus 2 are traditional British Sports cars, with a unique combination of performance and style. When the Elan first appeared, it was hailed as a quantum leap above its competition, with unmatched performance, handling, and roadholding, as well as striking good looks and a surprising level of practicality. Powered by Lotus' own engine, the model's then-unique sheet steel chassis and glass fibre bodyshell gave the car lightness, and the car's suspension relied on long, carefully damped travel to provide the Lotus' trademark road manners. When compared to the other small roadsters on the market, the Elan exhibits incredible levels of poise and balance, and shows how crude were the offerings from mainstream manufacturers. However, even with Chapman's genius behind it, the design of the Elan is still governed by the laws of physics, and its relatively skinny tyres do limit ultimate grip, when compared with today's offerings.

The Elan Coupé was introduced in 1965, bestowing the Elan with a good dose of refinement, without loss of performance.

The Elan and Plus 2's Lotus Twin-Cam engines are great units with a large amount of character (read: noise) inherent in their design, which adds to the driving experience. Performance is good for their age and engine size, and both will easily hold their own in modern traffic. The ride is surprisingly compliant, as roadholding and handling is achieved by having long travel, carefully controlled damping, and softish springing – all traits developed by Lotus from racing experiences and directly attributable to Colin Chapman. The brakes, with discs all round, are surprisingly modern in specification and, because they have such little weight to haul down from speed, work well.

As the Elan developed, the interiors got nicer. This is an Elan Series 2 with the full-width wooden dashboard.

The early Elan Series 1 and 2s have a typical no-nonsense British sports car cockpit, with relatively sparse furnishings, a wooden dashboard (full-width from the Series 2 cars), full instrumentation (speedo, rev counter, combined oil pressure and water temperature gauge, and a fuel gauge) along with rubber floor mats, a build-it-yourself hood, and manual 'pull-up' windows. From the Series 3 cars and the

Coupés, things got a bit more luxurious, with electric windows, carpeting and, for the dhc, a much better hood which could be pulled up and down quickly and easily. Small fresh-air vents at the extremity of the dash were fitted from the late Series 3 cars. The boot is a reasonable size and there is extra luggage space behind the seats, making the car practical as a tourer.

The first of the Plus 2 models' interior was a cut above that of the Elan, with a large veneered wooden dash hosting the speedo and rev counter opposite the driver, and four separate gauges for oil pressure, engine temperature, fuel level and battery charge in the centre console. A round 'eyeball' fresh-air vent was positioned at each end of the dash, and a decent heater was fitted with two-speed blower. The Plus 2S added an outside temperature gauge and clock to the centre console, as well as a passenger side map-reading light, giving the car what was probably the best-equipped dash at the time. The seats were plumped up to give more comfort, and standard electric windows and an efficient ventilation system made the Plus 2 a car capable of keeping its passengers comfortable in most conditions. The Plus 2's boot is a reasonable size, and while the rear seats are strictly for children, an adult can be accommodated cross-wise, with some contortions.

Spares for Elans and Plus 2s are in good supply, with many parts still being manufactured. Body repair panels are available, and so are complete replacement body shells and chassis. Service items and suspension bushes are all readily available, as are wheel bearings and suspension swivels. There are plenty of good Lotus clubs and web resources dedicated to the Elan and Plus 2, which make it much easier for new owners to get answers for questions, and to build up their knowledge of the car.

Today the Lotus Elan and Plus 2 are relatively rare classics, which will attract attention wherever they go, and give the owner superlative handling, roadholding and performance. Practical, economical and exhilarating to drive, relatively easy to maintain, and with a race-bred heritage, the Elan and Plus 2 are two of the best classic cars available today.

The frontal view of the Plus 2 is its most striking aspect. The long flat bonnet and nose and pop-up headlights are unlike those of any other car.

In producing the Coupé version of the Elan, Lotus managed to preserve the original car's good looks. Later Coupés like this one had an efficient through-flow ventilation system, as indicated by the extractor vents on the 'C' pillar.

4 Relative values
– which model for you?

Over 12 years of production, there have been numerous versions of the Elan and Plus 2. Starting with the Elan, there are seven basic models, five open-topped cars and three coupés. The open-topped cars comprise the Series 1, 2, 3, 4 and Sprint, while the coupés comprise Series 3, 4 and Sprint models. The Plus 2 started with the basic Plus 2 model, which was followed by the Plus 2S, then the Plus 2S 130, which was sold alongside the Plus 2S 130/5, which was fitted with the optional five-speed gearbox.

Model	Type	Lotus type	Production dates
Elan series 1	Convertible	Type 26	Jan 1962 to Nov 1964
Elan series 2	Convertible	Type 26	Nov 1964 to June 1966
Elan Coupé	Fixed-head coupé	Type 36	Sept 1965 to June 1966
Elan Series 3	Fixed-head coupé	Type 36	June 1966 to Mar 1968
Elan Series 3	Drophead coupé	Type 45	June 1966 to Mar 1968
Elan Super Safety	Drophead coupé	Type 45	1966 to 1968
Elan Series 4	Fixed-head coupé	Type 36	Mar 1968 to Oct 1970
Elan Series 4	Drophead coupé	Type 45	Mar 1968 to Oct 1970
Elan Sprint	Fixed-head coupé	Type 36	Oct 1970 to Aug 1973
Elan Sprint	Drophead coupé	Type 45	Oct 1970 to Aug 1973
Plus 2	Coupé	Type 50	Sept 1967 to Mar 1969
Plus 2S	Coupé	Type 50	Mar 1969 to Feb 1971
Plus 2 S 130	Coupé	Type 50	Feb 1971 to Dec 1974
Plus 2 S 130/5	Coupé	Type 50	Oct 1972 to Dec 1974

Price comparisons

In general, the Elan market is polarised between the early cars, many of which are eligible for various historic racing classes, and the final Sprints. This results in a price premium for Series 1s, Series 2s and Sprints, over and above the prices asked for Series 3 and 4 cars.

With the Plus 2, prices generally increase as the cars get younger, with the Plus 2S 130/5 generally commanding the highest prices.

The factory listed a hard top as an extra for the Series 1 and Series 2 Elans. This particular example was owned by the late Jim Clark.

However, all Plus 2 values are on the up and the price differential between the first and last cars is decreasing.

Note that in the Elan and Plus 2 market, there's an emerging trend for original cars, which are starting to see significant gains in value over good but unoriginal cars.

Elan Series 1

The Elan Series 1 Lotus Type 26, which was produced from October 1961, was only available as a convertible, and had separate rear lights (two round units on each side) and a single number plate light mounted on the top of the rear panel. The boot lid was set into the rear deck.

With the hood up, the Elan is still an attractive car. This Series 1 displays the large plastic rear windows and the tight fit that a good hood should exhibit. Note the boot lid recessed into the deck.

The interior was simple, with plastic mats on the floor, front-hinged seats and an oiled teak dashboard on the driver's side, which carried on to the centre console. The plain passenger side dash was taken up by an open glovebox. The windows slide up and down manually, using a small chrome clip in the top of the glass, and the hood had a removable cover with separate transverse rails and longitudinal glass fibre cant rails, which fitted over the doors. The engine produced 105bhp and the car had 5.20x13 crossply tyres as standard, while 145x13 radials were an option. The seats pivoted on their front mounting to adjust for length and height, and could hinge forwards to give access to the small luggage area at the rear of the cabin.

A racing version, the Type 26R, was introduced soon after the Elan was in production. Only about a hundred were produced originally. They featured tuned engines, a strengthened chassis and various suspension tweaks, including solid driveshafts with universal joints. Replicas are still being produced today to compete in the various historic racing classes, but that's outside the scope of this book.

Elan Series 2

The Series 2, still designated the Lotus Type 26, and still only available as a convertible, replaced the Series 1 in November 1964, and had a new full-width dashboard with chromed bezel instruments and a lockable glovebox. The separate rear lights were replaced with integrated units from Vauxhall (although, in typical early Lotus fashion, some early Series 2 cars retained the Series 1 arrangement). A quick-release fuel cap was fitted, as were larger front brake calipers.

The Series 2 SE was introduced in January 1966, and had a 115bhp engine, which was achieved by increasing the

The Series 2 differed only slightly from the Series 1 with a new dashboard and new rear lights.

compression ratio and fitting new camshafts. Knock-on steel wheels, close-ratio gearbox, brake servo and indicator repeater lights on the front wing were also fitted.

Elan Coupé

The first fixed-head coupé (fhc) version of the Elan, the Type 36, was introduced in September 1965, and did not have a 'Series' designation – it was simply known as the Elan Coupé. It had an all-new fixed-head coupé bodyshell, which included new flattened wheelarches, and redesigned and reshaped doors. The boot lid was extended over the rear panel to eliminate the drainage problems with the Series 1 and 2's recessed lid. A pair of number plate lights were mounted on the overhanging rear edge of the new boot moulding.

Electric windows were fitted with chromed window frames to give a good seal to the door, and the door a good seal to the body. A fully carpeted interior made it more comfortable.

The Elan Coupé had a new bodyshell, which had the boot lid overlapping the rear deck and revised wheelarches. The rear light clusters were sourced from the Vauxhall parts bin.

Elan Series 3

The Series 3 drophead coupé (dhc), Lotus Type 45, was introduced in June 1966. This took the Coupé bodyshell and replaced the fixed roof with an all-new hood, which had its frame permanently bolted to the bodyshell, and, when down, fitted virtually flush into the parcel shelf area behind the seats. The electric windows meant the chromed window surrounds of the Coupé were retained, giving a good fixed area for the hood to seal to.

This Elan Series 3 drophead coupé shows the new rear end, flattened wheelarches and door window frame that differentiate the model from the Series 2.

The Series 3 Coupé was introduced at the same time, and had a new through-flow ventilation system – identifiable by the rectangular grille covering vents in the rear 'B' pillar, just behind the door – which improved the driver environment. Both the Series 3 fhc and dhc gained small fresh-air vents on the outer extremities of the dash in December 1966. The SE specification could be applied to the Series 3 fhc and dhc.

Elan Super Safety

The Super Safety was an export version of the Series 3 for the US market, which was produced during 1966 and 1967. Produced in response to the new safety legislation introduced as a result of campaigning by US safety activist Ralph Nader, the Super Safety had passive safety features such as recessed door handles and instruments recessed into the dash. In some cases, rocker switches replaced toggle switches to make the car's interior safer for the driver and passenger. The seats were fitted with runners like the S4, but didn't tilt. It seems that most were supplied with bolt-on wheels, and those with knock-on wheels initially had special spinners with the three ears turned inwards, to avoid disembowelling an innocent passerby, although these were quickly replaced with octagonal 'Nader Nuts.' Most Super Safety cars were exported to the US, but there are some in the UK.

Elan Series 4

The Series 4 fhc (Type 36) and dhc (Type 45) were introduced in March 1968, and featured a number of detail changes, including the safety changes made to the Super Safety models. There were two types of S4; the Federal units, equipped with Stronberg CV carburetors and charge warming plumbing to meet US emissions standards, and the home and general export model, which came with Webers and later Dellortos, although some home market cars were also fitted with Strombergs. The most significant change was a revised bodyshell with flared wheelarches, which allowed for the fitting of wider 155x13 radial tyres as standard. The flares meant that the tops of both front and rear wheelarches were flattened further than seen on the Series 3 cars. The fhc and dhc shells were all produced from the same moulds, with the dhc losing the fixed roof. At the rear, new large rectangular rear light clusters, shared with the Plus 2 and similar to those seen on the Series 2 Jaguar E-Type, were fitted, along with revised number plate lights on the boot lid, which had slightly shortened hinges.

The dhc gained a new design of hood, and both cars' interiors had new trim in perforated vinyl, and new seats which could be adjusted, fore and aft,

The Elan Super Safety was essentially a Series 3 with some interior modification to improve the passive safety of the cockpit. It was aimed at the US market, and many of the safety modifications were carried over to the Series 4.

The Series 4 Elan had new rear lights and a slightly revised bodyshell to allow the fitment of wider tyres, as well as an uprated interior.

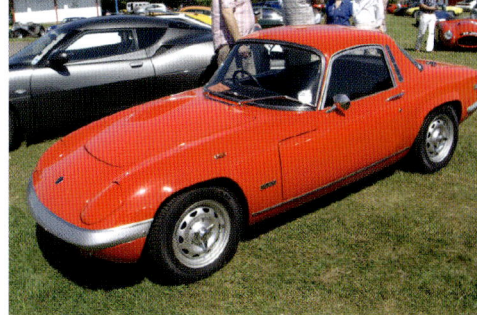

The Series 4 Coupé also gained the new wheelarches and improved interior trim. The same body moulds were used to produce the fhc and dhc.

by moving the seat on its runners. The new doors featured new interior panels, flush-fitting interior handles and outside handles with separate locks. The dash gained safety-conscious rocker switches and recessed instruments, and the bonnet pull became a single pull knob.

The bonnet gained a 'power bulge' to clear the Stromberg carburettors, but note that this bonnet was fitted even when Webers or Dellortos were fitted. The SE specification, with its 115bhp engine, 3.5:1 ratio differential, brake servo, knock-on wheels with chrome rim embellishments, carpeted boot and 'SE' badges, could be applied to both the Series 4 fhc and dhc. Finally, the electrical system was changed to the industry standard negative earth.

The final iteration of the Elan was the Sprint. Fitted with the 125bhp 'Big Valve' engine, it was the fastest standard Elan, and is much sought-after today.

Elan Sprint and Five-speed

The final iteration of the Elan was the Series 4 Sprint model, produced in dhc (Type 45) and fhc (Type 36). It was built from February 1971 through to the end of production in August 1973. The Sprint was fitted with the Big Valve Twin-Cam, which had larger diameter inlet valves and hotter 'Sprint' cams, giving a claimed 126bhp, and a significant boost in performance. A new cam cover was fitted to the Sprint engine with 'Lotus Big Valve' cast into the top front over the cam chain. Stronger Rotoflexes were fitted to the driveshafts, and the differential had a stiffening bracket bolted to the top of the casing. Externally, the Sprint had gold painted bumpers and black wheels, and two-tone paintwork as standard.

From the front quarter, the Plus 2's sleek lines can be appreciated. This early example has the optional Lotus alloy wheels.

The paint had the top colour starting at the waistline, and delineated from the lower colour with a gold stripe with 'Elan Sprint' written on it. Lotus did offer a single colour option to their customers, at an extra cost.

Elan Plus 2

The Plus 2 (all the Plus 2 models were designated Type 50) was a stretched and widened Elan, and it shared its overall layout and mechanical elements. Introduced in September 1967, the Plus 2 had an attractive, coupé style, two-door body, with, as the name suggests, two small child-friendly seats in the rear of the cabin. Placed in the market as a GT car, the Plus 2 was equipped with the 118bhp SE specification Twin-Cam engine as standard, and came with a good level of trim. This included a full-width veneered dash which, along with the speedometer and rev counter, sported four additional dials showing fuel level, oil pressure, engine temperature and battery condition. The Plus 2 gained a number of specification changes throughout its life, including the replacement of Italian Carello rear light units with Lucas units (shared with the Elan Series 4) after the first 160 or so cars, and the introduction of Federal compliant cars in March 1968, with new doors with flush interior handles, a new steering column and remote opening for the boot lid. When Stromberg carburettors were adopted in December 1968 for Federal cars, a new bonnet with power bulge was specified, which was used on most (if not all) of the subsequent cars, even when fitted with Webers or Dellortos.

Plus 2S

The Plus 2S was launched in March 1969 and was the first Lotus road car that was not available in kit form. The Plus 2S had a more luxurious interior, with a new '8 dial' dashboard, adding a clock and outside temperature gauge to the Plus 2's already comprehensive array of instruments. The seats were plumped up to make them more comfortable, rocker switches were fitted to the dash to meet safety legislation and the interior trim was improved with a new centre console. The most obvious exterior change was the fitting of rectangular fog lights under the front bumper.

The Plus 2's rear quarter is no less attractive. This early Plus 2 has the standard Lotus 'knock-on' steel wheels.

Plus 2 S130 and 130/5

The final iteration of the Plus 2 was the Plus 2S 130 and Plus 2S 130/5 which kept Lotus in the GT market until the introduction of the new lotus Elite in 1974. Launched in January 1971, the main change from the previous Plus 2S was the fitment of the Sprint specification Twin-Cam, which produced a claimed 126bhp when fitted with Weber or Dellortos, or 113bhp in Federal spec with Strombergs. The only exterior change was the option of a self-coloured silver metal flake roof. October 1972 saw the option of Lotus' own five-speed gearbox.

Only the badges give away that this Plus 2 is a last of the line Plus 2S 130/5, fitted with Lotus' own five-speed gearbox.

5 Before you view
– be well informed

Once you've found what appears to be a good car, it's well worth the effort to ask the vendor some searching questions, to ensure it's what you want to buy, and to avoid a wasted journey.

Where is the car?
The location of the car is significant, and a car near to you may be worth a look if only to build up your knowledge of the Elan or Plus 2, and give you a bench mark against which you can compare other cars. If the car is a long way away the costs of getting there, in terms of travel and time, may be significant.

This lovely early Series 4 Elan with its roll bar is fully equipped for track days.

Dealer or private sale
Establish if the car is being sold by the owner or by a dealer. If it's a private sale by the owner, then you have little legal recourse if you buy the car and subsequently find problems with it (in the UK, it's very much a case of 'caveat emptor' or buyer beware). If you buy from a dealer in the UK, you will get a significant level of legal protection, and usually a warranty or guarantee of sorts. Owners should be able to provide you with details of the car's history in both written and verbal form. Dealers will probably have a paper history file, but will not have as much knowledge about the car's history.

Early Elans are sought-after, and this Series 1 appears to be in excellent condition.

Cost of collection and delivery
It's worth working out collection and delivery costs, especially if the car is a long way away. Even if you're proposing to drive the car home, you still need to get to the vendor's site. The cost of having the car transported to your base may be cheaper than you expect if you use a web-based courier/car collection portal, which you can find by searching for 'car shipping' on the web. There are many companies that specialise in moving cars on low loaders, which offer surprisingly reasonable rates.

Viewing: when and where?
When viewing any car, it's important to go to the seller's address, or the business premises of the vendor. If they suggest meeting in a public area, like a car park or motorway services, treat this with caution as it could make it difficult to trace

the vendor if problems arise. If you view the car at a private seller's home, make sure the documentation is in the vendor's name and is the same as the viewing address; for a business sale, the vendor should have the registration documentation. View the car in daylight, and give yourself plenty of time to carry out the checks outlined below. Be very careful if it's raining because a wet car can conceal poor paintwork.

The Plus 2's expansive rear screen gives great rearward visibility. This late Plus 2S is painted in traditional Lotus yellow.

Reason for sale
Ask the seller why they are selling and how long they have owned the car. There are many legitimate reasons and it's alway worth seeing if the answer is plausible.

Left-hand drive to right-hand drive
Ask if the car has been converted to right-hand drive (or vice versa) and if so, was the conversion done professionally? While the Elan and Plus 2 are relatively easy to convert, it does compromise originality.

Condition (body, chassis, mechanical, interior)
Ask the vendor for a description of the condition of the car, and ask if there are any problems. While the seller's opinion of what is 'good condition' may be different to yours, most sellers are honest and will give you an idea of what to expect.

This is a lovely example of a Series 4 fhc. Some Coupés have had their roofs cut off to convert them to dropheads; this example has avoided that fate.

All original specification
Ask if the car is verifiably original. Is it in the same colour it left the factory, and does it have the original engine, chassis, interior and bodyshell? What modifications have been done to the car? Does the owner have a Lotus Heritage certificate to confirm the original factory specification, and unit and engine numbers?

Chassis and engine numbers
Do the chassis/VIN and engine numbers on the car match the registration document and (if available) a Lotus Heritage certificate? If not, ask why.

Matching data/legal
For a private sale, ask if the car is owned by the vendor, and if the vendor's name and address is on the registration document. If not, ask why and verify the

The Plus 2 makes a fine touring car. This example shows how the traditional Lotus yellow suits the sleek lines of the car.

answer, for example, if the vendor is selling the car on behalf of a third party, ask to be put in touch with them. If the car is being sold by the vendor, ask to see some identification to verify that the vendor is who he or she says he or she is.

In the UK, the DVLA (via the website gov.uk) offers various checks based on a vehicle's registration number – this free online service can be useful to check that the car is what it's supposed to be – if you run the registration number, the make and colour of the car can be confirmed. The MOT status of the car can also be seen, and the site will allow you to look at the car's MOT history since 2005.

In the UK, there are a number of companies that will carry out checks on vehicles based on the registration number. The checks can identify if the vehicle has been stolen, if it's an insurance write-off, and if there is outstanding finance on the car.

Unleaded fuel
The Elan and Plus 2 engine was built with cast iron valve seats cast into its alloy head. The general consensus is that the cars will run happily on unleaded fuel, but high revs can cause valve seat recession. For total peace of mind, there are additives available, or companies who will replace the existing valve seats with new ones.

Insurance
Before you can drive the car on the road in the UK, you must have insurance in place. Many insurance companies can pre-arrange cover and then activate it to a new owner over the phone. If you take the car out for a test drive, make sure you're covered.

How you can pay
Ask the vendor how they want you to pay. Cash is king, and waving a wad of notes will often get you a discount, but bank transfers, cheques and bank drafts are all safer than carrying a large amount of cash. Most sellers will want to make sure the funds have cleared before releasing the car.

Buying at auction
See chapter 10 for details.

Professional vehicle check (mechanical examination)
If you don't feel you have the skills or confidence to carry out a mechanical inspection, there are organisations and individuals who can do so for a fee. There are motoring organisations in most countries (such as the AA and RAC in the UK) which will carry out vehicle checks, but in the case of a specialist classic car like the Elan and Plus 2, you would be better off going to a marque specialist or engaging a knowledgable friend to inspect the car.

This Plus 2 engine bay is very tidy. The Weber carburettors still sport their standard air box, which connects to the air filter positioned in the nose of the car via the large diameter pipe snaking around the radiator.

6 Inspection equipment
– these items will really help

This book
Reading glasses (if you need them for close work).
Notebook and pencil (to jot down information as you inspect the car).
Overalls (to protect your clothes and to show you mean business).
Trolley jack, blocks of wood, chocks and axle stands (use the wood blocks to prevent damage to the car when you jack it up. Use the front chassis crossmember or the factory jacking points and make sure you don't damage the car. Make sure you chock the wheels to stop the car rolling off the jack, and use the axle stands to ensure that if the jack fails the car is still supported).
Fridge magnet and strong magnet on telescopic stick (these will be no use in assessing the integrity of the glass fibre bodyshell, but they should be used on the various points where the chassis is exposed, to make sure it's all metal).
Torch or head torch and a handheld LED light (the torch should be one that gives you a focused beam of light to allow you to peer into tight spots, such as the gaps between the bodyshell and the chassis, while the handheld LED lamp or head torch should give a brilliant spread of light, that will hopefully make peering under the car and in wheelarches easier).
Digital camera/camera phone (to take pictures of inaccessible areas, areas you're not sure about and may need to research further, and the VIN plate and registration document, so you can research the car's numbers at your leisure).
Mirror on a stick (to look at relatively inaccessible areas).
Probe – a small screwdriver is ideal (to have a poke at anything that looks suspicious, such as parts of the chassis that look corroded).
Small pry bar or large screwdriver (to check for excessive play in suspension bushes and swivels).
Stethoscope or long screwdriver (to locate where any strange noises in the engine are coming from; use the long screwdriver by placing the handle against your ear and the blade on the engine, where you think the noise is coming from – beware of moving parts).
Engine compression tester and plug spanner (to assess the engine's overall condition and identify problems with individual cylinders).
A friend or marque specialist (to give you a second opinion on any immediate queries, give you an objective, unemotional view of the car and help you decide if it's the one for you).

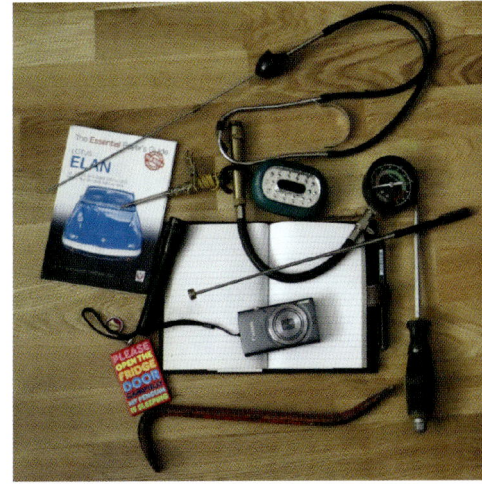

A selection of tools and accessories you should take with you when inspecting a car.

7 Fifteen minute evaluation
– walk away or stay?

Introduction
This initial inspection should take around 15 minutes, and will tell you if the car is what it says it is, if it's in the condition that warrants further scrutiny, and if you think it might be the car for you. Try to see the car with a cold engine, so when it's started you can hear any knocks or rattles, and see if it starts easily when cold. Also, a cold engine makes it a lot easier to assess the outside state of the engine and cooling system, as you won't burn your hands on hot components.

The owner and numbers check
Check the Vehicle Identification Number (VIN) and engine number. These will be in the car's documentation, and those on the car's VIN plate and engine should match the paperwork. If they don't, and the vendor doesn't have a good reason why, don't buy the car. If you're buying from an individual, their name and address should be on the registration document. Ask to see their driving licence and view the car at the given address. If they don't match or something isn't right, walk away.

If the car is a dhc but has the Type 36 designation in the VIN (see chapter 17 for the VIN formats), the car came out of the factory as a Coupé and has been converted to dhc specification, which detracts from its originality.

The car VIN, and sometimes the engine number, are scratched or stamped on a data plate, usually mounted on the bodywork in the left-hand side of the engine bay. The Twin-Cam's engine number is stamped on the engine block, above the carburettor side engine mount. There may be a chassis number stamped on the front upper face of the chassis, above the engine mount, and a body number moulded into the front edge of the top of the bonnet, opening in the engine bay, but these are internal Lotus numbers and probably won't match the car's VIN.

There are a number of companies that will carry out data checks on a car for a small fee. While they're usually used on newer cars to check for outstanding finance, they will show if a car has been stolen or written-off. A Lotus Heritage certificate should give the original numbers, paint colour and ex-factory date.

The VIN plate is in the engine bay in right-hand drive Elans.

In the Plus 2, the VIN plate is in the forward end of the engine bay.

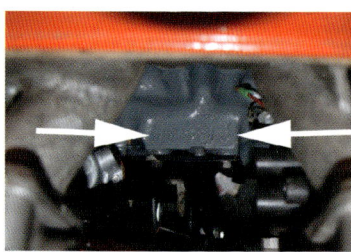

The Twin-Cam engine's number is stamped onto a platform on the centre of the side of the block below the carburettors. The number can be difficult to make out.

The walk around

Take your time to walk around the car and look for any problems. This stage should be used to identify any obvious damage or faults with the exterior of the car.

Is the paint dull or nicely polished? Does it have any major blistering or micro blisters? Is it all the same shade? If there are pinstripes, are they all there? If the car has recently been resprayed, ask for evidence that it's been done correctly.

There's nothing obviously wrong with the exterior of this Plus 2 or the yellow coupé behind it.

Does the car sit square to the ground, or is one side or corner lower than the other? Are the wheels square in their arches, with equal gaps between the tyres and bodyshell, and are the gaps the same on each side? Do the wheels have the same camber on each side? If not, further investigation is needed.

Do the doors, bonnet and boot lids fit with even panel gaps? On Series 4 Elans, the doors rarely fit properly, and the bottom rear edge is often slightly proud of the bodywork. Do they open cleanly, without drooping? Do the locks and catches work smoothly and close easily? Are there any gaps where the doors meet the door seals?

Is the brightwork present and in good condition? While there isn't much on the Elan Series 1 and 2, the 3 and 4s and Plus 2s had chromed surrounds on their electric side windows. The Plus 2 has chromed bumpers – check they're dent and rust-free, with good chrome. Check that the windscreen is free of cracks and scratches, and that the windscreen wipers are in good condition. If it's an Elan Coupé or a Plus 2, is there a sunroof? If so, is it original or aftermarket? Lotus didn't fit sunroofs at the factory, but a folding vinyl type roof was a dealer-fitted option. Aftermarket tinted glass lift-out 'moon' roofs were popular in the '80s and '90s, but can be prone to leaks. Are the rear lights correct for the car? There should be small round lights on the Series 1 and early Series 2, Vauxhall one-piece units on later Series 2 and 3, and larger oblong Lucas units on the Series 4, Sprint and Plus 2. The first 160 Plus 2s had smaller one-piece Carello rear lights. Check the lenses are crack-free and not crazed.

The interior

Early Elan Series 1 or 2 interiors had just enough room for a couple of passengers and the controls and instruments. Later Elans and Plus 2s had more creature comforts, so there's more to check. Inside the car, does it smell musty or damp? Are the carpets or mats worn or damp? Are the seat covers split? Is the hood all there and is the plastic rear window undamaged? Are all the instruments present, working, and in good condition? If it's a coupé or a Plus 2, is

Early Elan interiors (this is a Series 2) have minimal fixtures and fittings, but are still nicely trimmed and should be pretty tidy.

The Plus 2 is more luxurious than the basic Elan, with much more equipment and trim. This is a Plus 2 with the four minor instrument dash. The plus 2S had six minor instruments on the dash.

the headlining in good condition? Finally, check the door trim and operation of the windows. The Series 1 and 2 Elans have counterbalanced manual 'pull-up' windows, which should move easily and smoothly, and should stay put when opened or closed. The later Elans and Plus 2s have electric windows, which should work smoothly, if not particularly quickly.

Under the bonnet

Under the bonnet, the engine bay should be clean and tidy, with neat wiring and no evidence of obvious mistreatment. Take a look for any evidence of accident damage to the bodyshell while poking about under the bonnet: while this isn't a problem if it's been repaired properly, any repairs should be neat and unobtrusive, with minimal filler.

With Dellorto carbs and 'Big Valve' engine, this is a late Plus 2S 130 engine bay. Note the Dellorto carburettors and standard air box.

Using this book, make sure everything that should be there is there: for example, air boxes and filters are often discarded in the search for better performance. Does the car have the right carburettors? All home market Elans and Plus 2s came with a pair of twin-choke Webers up to around 1969, and then could have been fitted with a pair of Stromberg CV carburettors. Home and general export market cars reverted to Webers in 1971, and then twin-choke Dellortos were fitted as standard in 1972. All US Federal emissions-equipped cars came with Strombergs, and had 'crossover' plumbing to preheat the charge to reduce emissions. On the Twin-Cam engine, the inlet manifold is part of the head casting, so swapping from Strombergs to Webers or Dellortos means changing the head: Dellortos and Webbers are interchangeable. The Twin-Cam can be somewhat incontinent, so expect to see oil in the engine bay, though it shouldn't be awash. Cam cover leaks aren't uncommon, and may indicate a warped cam cover, or if the oil is around the fixing nuts on the top of the cover, then the wrong (or no) sealing washers have been used, but there should not be any leakage from the head gasket or the timing chain case. Check the engine is cold, then look under the radiator cap to see if the coolant is clean and up to the correct level. Check for white 'mayonnaise' on the underside of the oil filler cap – this implies a leaking head gasket – and take out the dip stick and look at the oil: is it clean, above the minimum level marking, and are there any metallic particles in it, which implies problems with the bearings?

Feel (carefully) if the engine is cold before asking the owner to start it. Listen closely for heavy knocks, indicating serious main or big end bearing wear, and lighter top end noise, indicating out of adjustment or worn tappets. A rattle from the front of the unit indicates timing chain wear. Ticking from the top end indicates loose valve clearances. The unit should settle down to a steady, even tickover fairly quickly.

This Plus 2 is sitting nicely, with correct gaps between the wheels and arches, front and rear. Make sure the one you are viewing has the same stance.

The intangibles

While carrying out this inspection of the car, you should be forming some opinions about it. Has it been well kept? Does it have the correct documentation? Could you live with it? If not, there are plenty more out there, and you should walk away.

8 Key points
– where to look for problems

With the Elan and Plus 2, you must pay particular attention to the following areas:

Body
The bodyshell of an Elan or Plus 2 will be corrosion-free, but there are often problems with the paintwork, and stress cracking in the gel coat. If there's obvious evidence of accident damage or other repairs to the body, they haven't been done properly and will need to be redone. The bodyshell has steel reinforcement, which is bonded in around the doors in the Elan, and in the Plus 2 comprises box section steel members in the sills, which also incorporate the outer seatbelt mounts; these can rust.

Chassis
The original Lotus chassis is made from relatively thin gauge sheet steel and can rust, especially at the front and the central backbone.

The chassis is also vulnerable to misalignment due to crash damage. In general, the front and rear suspension should operate quietly, smoothly and compliantly – hard or sagging springs and worn dampers or bushes will have a significant effect on the car's ride and handling. The front suspension bottom trunnions are prone to seizure if they are not regularly lubricated. At the rear, the lower tubular wishbone can be bent if used to jack the car up, and rear wheel bearings are weak and need regular replacement. The car is prone to vibration when rolling, if the wheels are out of balance.

The Elan's chassis is made from relatively thin gauge sheet steel and can rust. This rolling chassis has been fully restored.

Engine
On the Twin-Cam engines, the water pump and timing chain are the two main wearing items. Check that the timing chain adjuster still has some adjustment on it, the water pump bearings are good and smooth, and there are no leaks from around the pump. The Twin-Cam is also prone to oil leakage. While light leakage (usually from the cam cover gasket) is acceptable and helps to protect the centre section and the rear of the

Up-front, this Plus 2 chassis shows the suspension turrets (1), the front crossmember which is also used as a vacuum reservoir for the pop-up headlamps (2), the perforated platform for mounting the steering rack (3) and the four wishbone mounting spindles (4).

chassis from rust, copious amounts of oil outside of the engine is not a good sign.

Transmission

All the forward gears on the Elan and Plus 2 gearbox had synchromesh as standard, so make sure it still operates. The Lotus five-speed box, which is standard on the Plus 2S 130/5 and very few Sprints, is not the most reliable of units. Watch out for bearing noise, weak synchromesh on any gear, popping out of gear and poor shift action.

At the rear of the car there can be problems with the driveshafts. It's hard to find good quality Rotoflex rubber joints, and if they fail while the car is being driven, a driveshaft could potentially flail around and penetrate the passenger compartment. Later driveshafts have a tubular extension, which prevents the driveshaft escaping from between the differential and the hub, should a Rotoflex fail catastrophically.

Electrical

Electrical problems and glass fibre cars go hand-in-hand, as the system has many more earth leads and connections than a steel car, resulting in lots of extra potential problems.

Any fire in a glass fibre car can rapidly spread, due to the inflammable nature of the bodyshell, and while repairs are perfectly possible if a fire gets hold, the car may well burn out. Electrical fires are not uncommon, so pay particular attention to the electrics, looking for loose wires, poorly secured looms, missing grommets where wires pass through the body, frayed or worn insulation and dodgy connections. Note that on the Twin-Cam engine, the distributor lives below the carburettors, so any fuel leaks can be disastrous.

At the front of the timing cover is the water pump (blue arrow) and on the side is the cam chain tensioner (yellow arrow).

Early (left) and late Rotoflex rubber donuts. Carefully inspect any on the car carefully for splits and cracks. New, good quality ones are expensive, and cheap ones do not last.

The engine bay of a long-derelict Plus 2. It all needs to be stripped out and replaced.

9 Serious evaluation
– 60 minutes for years of enjoyment

Introduction
You've carried out the fifteen minute evaluation and the car is looking good. So it's time to get down and dirty and carry out an in-depth appraisal, to see if the car is actually what you want to buy, and what overall condition it's in. The detailed inspection should be carried out methodically, and don't let the vendor distract you from carrying out all the checks.

When you inspect the front and rear suspension, you'll need to have the car jacked up. On the Elan, the standard jack has a 'U' shaped crutch, which should slot onto the flange on the bottom of the sill. Positioning the jack just in front of the rear edge of the door will result in both wheels on the side being lifted clear of the ground. The Plus 2 has jacking points at each end of the sill, between the wheels. The standard Plus 2 jack has a vertical stud which is located in a hole in the sill, inside of which there should be a pressed steel box section, with brackets that receive the jack. These box sections can rust, and should not be trusted unless they've recently been renewed. Lifting an Elan or Plus 2 using a trolley jack can be achieved at the front by using the front crossmember of the chassis, and at the rear on each side of the rear of the floorpan next to the sill, while using a block of wood to spread the load. Never jack an Elan or Plus 2 up using the rear element of the chassis, or worse still, the rear wishbones, as this will cause damage. Never rely on the jack alone to support the body, alway use axle stands or other suitable supports to avoid the car falling unexpectedly.

Paintwork 4 3 2 1
Inspect the paintwork closely. It's easy to do a quick respray on a glass fibre car, which will look good for a little while (the classic 'resale red' finish), but a good paint job on a glass fibre car takes time and experience, and time and experience cost money. If the car's been resprayed recently, ask to see receipts, and make sure the bodyshop knows how to treat glass fibre repairs. See chapter 14 for the main problems encountered with paintwork.

Apart from the usual paint issues of fading, oxidation and poor colour matching of repairs, there are two extra features that the paintwork on glass fibre cars can exhibit. The gel coat can crack, usually around stress points such as door handles, locks, or where the bodywork has received a knock, resulting in a crack that goes through the paint, into the bodyshell itself. Poorly repaired gel coat cracks will reappear rapidly, and poor repairs will be exposed by the paint 'sinking' into them, leaving the outline of the repaired damage visible.

Extreme paintwork problems: stress cracks and some blistering, along with severely degraded paint.

Blistering of the paint can occur, and can, in fact, be transitory. It can be caused by osmosis – the process of moisture permeating through the paint and gel coat and then reacting with resin and matt layers – often as the result of leaving the car in a damp environment. The blisters will vary in size, from 2-5mm in diameter. The blistering may not crack the paint, and drying out the car may make the blisters disappear. However, they will reappear when the car next gets damp. Micro blistering means tiny blisters, almost pinprick sized, under the paint. Sometimes you can feel them by running your hand over the affected panel, or they may become visible by looking obliquely at the surface. Again, these are usually caused by moisture, but they can also be caused by the thinners in the paint itself, when sprayed. In either case, rectification is not difficult, but it will take time and it can be expensive to repair properly.

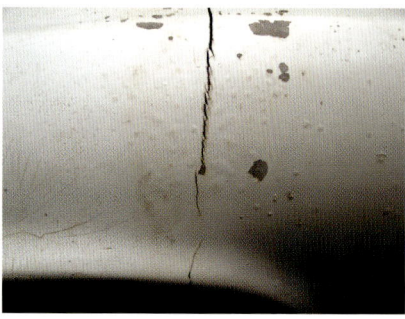

If a new panel hasn't been properly grafted on, you'll be able to see the join. This is a poorly-executed replacement front corner on a Plus 2, and the join above the front wheel arch is clearly visible.

Bodyshell 4 3 2 1

Major repairs to the bodyshell may not be obvious, as serious damage should have been repaired by cutting out the affected panel and scarfing in a new one. This type of repair is fine, as long as it's done properly. If, for example, a new front quarter has been fitted, you may feel a join under the wheelarch where the lower edges of old and new are joined, but you should not be able to see any evidence of the repair on top. If you can see evidence of a repair through the paintwork, then the repair is poor and needs redoing.

Series 4s and Sprints are renowned for their ill-fitting doors. 'They all do that, sir,' but careful hinge adjustment may improve the fit.

Minor repairs which have been done properly won't be visible, so if you can see evidence of any repairs through paint sinkage, rough areas or obvious joins, then these haven't been done properly and will need to be reworked or redone.

Check also for stress cracks which can form around hinges, door handles, on the surface of the doors, around the windscreen wiper pivots and around door locks, and anywhere else on the shell, if it's been hit.

The doors should fit nicely with reasonable panel gaps, and should be tight against the door seals when closed. However, on Series 4s and Sprints, the bottom rear edge of the doors were often poorly fitting from the factory. This is normal and nothing to worry about, but careful and meticulous adjustment can improve the fit. Check for door droop, which indicates worn hinge bushes, by lifting the open edge of the door and checking for play; it should be minimal.

The bonnet and boot will appear to be a bit floppy when opened. This is nothing to worry about, but both should sit flush with the surrounding bodywork when closed, and the boot lid should sit nicely on the rubber seals around the luggage compartment. This is important to ensure there are no water leaks into the boot. On the Series 1 and 2 Elans, the boot lid is recessed into the top panel, and has drainage holes connected by tubes to the boot floor. These are designed to drain water from the boot lid recess, and it's worth checking that they're present, clear of obstructions and the tubing is firmly attached, otherwise water will sit in the boot lid recess and eventually get into the boot.

The Elan has a 'u' shaped set of reinforcements, made from a lattice of steel rods, moulded into the bodyshell around each door opening. Check the inside of the shell behind the trim to make sure the steel rods aren't corroding – if water has got in, the steel will rust and expand, and 'blow' the glass fibre that holds the steel in place. It's not a disaster if it's rusted, but it's a fiddly and time-consuming job to cut out the old steel and replace it.

The Plus 2 has box section steel members concealed in the sills. These are hard to inspect without some dismantling, but are very important for the structural integrity of the vehicle, as they provide the jacking points and the lower outboard seatbelt mounting points. If the owner is nervous about using the 'official' jacking points at each end of the sill, this should raise suspicions. Each sill member is secured in the sill by three steel plates on the inside edge, which are bolted through the sill to the member with four bolts. These plates are under the carpet on the inside edge of the sill, and if they're rusty, so are the members. The middle plate also has the seatbelt mount on it, so the condition of the sills is vital for safety. As with the Elan, if the sills are rotten, it's a fiddly and time-consuming job to replace them.

The Series 1 and 2 boot lids sit flush in a recess in the rear deck. Check that the drain holes and pipes in the recess are clear, otherwise water will run past the seal and into the boot.

The Plus 2 has steel reinforcement beams concealed in its sills. These are bolted in place via three steel plates on the inner sill — the front two are arrowed. If the plates are rusty, the sill members will be badly rusted.

Chassis

The chassis is the heart of the car, and it can rust. In order to inspect it, you need to get under the car and have a really good poke about. If there's corrosion, the rear half of the chassis is usually better than the front, as it benefits from the gentle flow of oil back from the engine. At the front of the chassis, the main points to inspect are the turrets that carry the front suspension. There are drain holes on the bottom of the turret and these should be clear – if they're blocked, expect the worst. On early cars, the headlamps operate on a 'Fail Unsafe' mode, and are held up by vacuum. The front crossmember of the chassis is used as a vacuum tank, so if the lights are up and the engine is off, the lights should slowly sink back down; if they drop down almost immediately, there is either a leak in the system, or the crossmember has a leak in it, most likely due to corrosion.

The later 'Fail Safe' system relies on the vacuum to hold the lights down, so the lights should retract almost immediately when the engine is turned on – again, if they don't then either the system has a leak or the crossmember is corroded. Also, look for cracks around the engine mounts and at the rear where the differential tie rods bolt to the sides of the chassis. Take a close look at the areas of the chassis that are visible, the bottom of the central box under the centre of the car, the ends and bottom of the crossmember at the front, and the cross sections at the rear. If you find any corrosion, it will be worse in the areas you can't see. If the owner claims the car has had a new chassis, you want to see evidence of purchase. In extreme cases of rust in the chassis, the front turret can be so weakened that it bends inwards, cracking the bodyshell where it's mounted to the top of the turret. This sort of damage is easily spotted as the top of the front wheel will be tucked into the wheelarch. The body is bolted to the chassis and it's perfectly possible for a mechanically competent owner to remove the body from the chassis.

Lights & exterior trim

Luckily, there's little exterior trim on the Elan and Plus 2. On all the lights and indicators, make sure that the plastic lenses are not cracked or damaged, the chrome reflectors around the bulbs are

The front turrets on the Lotus chassis are hollow and open to the elements. If the drain hole (arrowed) is blocked, the turret bottoms will rot.

While the chassis rusts mainly at the front, the centre and rear sections can also rot. This Plus 2 chassis has some surface rust on the centre box which is easily treated and not terminal.

The rear of the Elan and Plus 2 chassis has two towers to pick up the top mounts of the Chapman struts. The holes for the top differential rubber mounts are visible on the top of the crossmember.

still shiny and doing their job, and that the chrome of the base plinths is in good condition, as these are made from the soft zinc-based alloy Mazak, and are almost impossible to rechrome.

On the Plus 2, check the condition of the roof gutter trim; some are alloy and others are chrome-plated brass. Also check the condition of the trim strips on the top of the door, just below the window, and the trim strip along the sill, just below the door.

The bumpers should follow the lines of the body closely. The Elan's painted glass fibre units should be crack-free, and the Plus 2's steel chromed units should be dent-free, with the chrome in good condition. On the Plus 2 and Series 3 onwards Elans, check that the chrome trim around the windows and the window rubbers are in good condition.

Wheels & tyres 4 3 2 1

Series 1 and 2 Elans had bolt-on steel wheels, but there was the option of Lotus knock-on steel wheels. These were standard on the SE models, and were fitted to most post Series 2 cars. The bolt-on steel wheels should have chromed hub caps with an embossed Lotus badge in its centre that covers the nuts. Standard tyre fitment for Series 1 and 2 Elans were 520x13 crossplys, with 145x13 radials as an option. Series 3 Elans came with 145x13 radials. The Series 4s and Sprints still had bolt-on wheels as a standard fitment, but most appear to have been equipped with knock-ons as standard, and wore 155x13 radials. The Plus 2 was fitted with two types of centre lock steel wheels, both fitted with 165x13 radials. The first type were painted silver, and some had press-on chromed rims. The second type had the outer rim chromed and the inner disc painted black. Later Plus 2Ss had optional Brand Lotus, eight-spoke alloy wheels made by GKN, which were 13in diameter with 5½in width, but were still fitted with 165x13 tyres. Aftermarket wheels are not uncommon, mainly of the Minilite persuasion.

The later (Series 4 and Plus 2 onwards) rear light units are available new; as are the lenses.

On the Plus 2, the front side lights are unique to the model. While new ones are available, they are not cheap. New lenses are available separately.

Lotus' own steel knock-on wheels feature on many Elans and Plus 2s. Note that the cutouts in the dish of the wheel mimic the shape of the Lotus logo.

Tyres should be in good condition, with decent tread and no cuts or tears in the sidewalls. It's worth checking the date code to see how old the tyres are. Classics often only rack up a low yearly mileage, and tyres deteriorate with age. All tyres produced since the year 2000 have a code moulded into the sidewall which starts with the letters 'DOT.' It includes a four-digit number: the first two denote the week of manufacture; the last two the year. So 2210 would indicate the tyre was made in week 22 of 2010. If there's a three-digit number, the tyre was produced before 2000 and should be replaced. It's recommended that tyres are replaced at 8-10 years old, so budget for a new set if this is the case.

Front suspension

The front suspension uses Triumph Spitfire/Vitesse uprights, disc brakes, top swivel joints, bottom brass trunnions, and Lotus wishbones. While it's on the ground, visually inspect the wheel for any damage and for any excessive camber, ie the wheel not sitting at 90 degrees to the road with the top or bottom leaning in or out.

Bounce each corner of the car to test the damper; the car should rise back up to its normal level, with no oscillating, if the dampers are in good condition. With the car jacked up, take the wheel and spin it. It should spin cleanly, with no in-and-out or up-and-down movement of the rim; if there is, the wheel is buckled. The wheel should also spin quietly and smoothly; if not, the wheel bearings need attention. Next, take the wheel by the top and bottom (12 and 6 o'clock) and try to rock it. There should be virtually no play; if there is then the wheel bearing,

Lotus own-brand ten-spoke knock-on alloy wheels were optional on the Plus 2, though many cars were supplied with them.

The date code for tyres is shown between the two arrows — in this case the code reads '4714,' showing that the tyre was produced during the 47th week of 2014.

This bare Elan rolling chassis shows the layout of the twin wishbone front suspension, the steering rack mounting, and the space between the chassis members for the engine.

top swivel or bottom trunnion, or the wishbone bushes on the chassis, may be worn, or the wheel nuts are loose. Check for play in the steering rack or trackrod ends and wheel bearings by taking the wheel at three and nine o'clock and rocking it. Take the wheel off and check the back of the wheel for any corrosion, dents or damage. Then inspect all the joints on the suspension and wishbones, levering them with a screwdriver or pry bar if necessary, to check for play. The next

This Plus 2 Spyder chassis shows the front suspension in detail.

check is to see if there's any up and down movement on the bottom trunnion by pulling up on the hub while feeling if there's any movement of the upright relative to the brass body of the trunnion. Check the rubber bushes connecting the front anti-roll bar to the suspension. The top bushes are on the front of the wishbone spindle on the chassis and the lower bushes are on the bottom shock absorber mount. The spring and damper unit should show no signs of oil leakage, and its top and bottom rubber mounts should be unworn. While the wheel is off, see the front brake inspection checks below. While your head is in the wheel well, check the glass fibre bodywork for any damage, and the chassis turrets for damage or corrosion, and check that the drain holes are clear.

Front brakes

Check that the front disc isn't scored or warped, or doesn't have an obvious wear ridge on its outside edge.

The thickness of an early new disc is 10mm, with a minimum of 9mm when worn out. Later cars discs were 13mm with a minimum thickness of 11mm. If the disc has corrosion on one side, it indicates that the relevant piston in the caliper is sticking and the caliper needs a rebuild. There should be no sign of any fluid leaking from the caliper, and check the thickness of the pads. The flexible hose to the caliper should be free of any cracks or leaks.

Steering rack

You've checked for play in the rack and the trackrod ends already, and the final check is to inspect the state of the rack's rubber bellows on the front of the chassis. The rack is rubber mounted to the lip on the front of the chassis crossmember; inspect the mounts for any signs of accident damage, wear in the

The front twin piston brake caliper is mounted behind the axle centre line. While this is a Plus 2, the Elan setup is the same.

rubber, or misalignment. Aftermarket kits are available to replace the rubber with solid mounts.

Rear suspension

At the rear repeat the checks specified under front suspension to check the dampers and the wheel for obvious misalignment, warpage or wheel bearing wear. Then jack the corner up and repeat the tests for play in the wheel bearings. Remove the wheel and check the back of the wheel for any corrosion, dents or damage.

The lower wishbone has two mounts to the chassis, and is through-bolted to the front and rear of the hub casting. There should be minimal play in the wishbone bushes onto the chassis and the hub – standard fit is metalastic but it's common to use poly bushes. The wishbone is a one-piece item made from lengths of tube, all of which should be straight – often cars are jacked up on the wishbone which will bend them, and kerbing can result in bends too. Check the wishbone lengths with a straight edge to confirm all is OK. The suspension top mount is rubber and should allow a small amount of side to side movement of the strut, to allow for the suspension to go up and down. This should be very small; excessive movement means the top mount is worn or perished. Check the strut for oil leaks from the damper.

Rear brakes

The rear brakes on the Elan and Plus 2 are discs, with the disc semi inboard sitting behind the hub casing, and the caliper mounted on the back of the hub casting. Check the disc has no run out, and that there is minimal wear – a new

The Elan and Plus 2 rear calipers are bolted onto the rear of the hub carriers. The mechanical handbrake mechanism and its operating rod are visible in the lower half of the shot.

The front of a Plus 2 Spyder chassis, with the engine installed. Note the circular section front crossmember and the tight fit of the engine.

At the rear, the Elan's differential is bolted in, but there are no driveshafts. The semi inboard rear discs, wide spaced lower wishbones and Chapman Struts are all clearly visible.

disc should be 9-10mm thick. Check the caliper for leaks, the pads for wear and the flexible hose for any damage, bulges or cracks.

The handbrake operates a pair of extra pads on the bottom of each rear brake caliper. It's operated by a pair of rods (one each side) that are pulled by the handbrake cable via a tree arrangement mounted on the chassis behind the differential.

The Elan's handbrake is renowned for its poor performance, but it's worth making sure it works by getting someone to put it on and off and observing the movement of the mechanism, and trying to turn the hub when the handbrake is on.

Driveshafts & differential

While the rear wheel is off, take a close look at the driveshaft. Firstly, ascertain what type of driveshaft is fitted – the standard rubber Rotoflex type, Spyder sliding shaft type with one universal joint and one Rotoflex, 26R type with sliding shaft and two universal joints, or CV type with two Constant Velocity joints and a sliding shaft. While there are no wearing parts in the Rotoflex coupling, look at them closely to make sure the rubber is in good condition, with no cracks, and still firmly attached to the moulded-in steel reinforcements. With CV shafts, rotate the shafts and listen for any clicks or clonks indicating worn CVs, and inspect

This Plus 2 rear suspension shot shows the CV-style driveshaft as well as the rear caliper and handbrake rod.

the CV boots for splits or leaking grease. With Universal Joints, look for any rust stains around them which indicates wear, and hold onto one flange and try to rotate and wriggle the other side to detect any play; there should be none. While you're under the rear of the car, if the standard Rotoflex type driveshafts are fitted, it's worth checking if they're later types with a tubular extension on each end, which is supposed to prevent the driveshaft coming adrift, should the Rotoflex fail.

Differentials are strong and rarely give trouble, but the mounts are susceptible to wear and oil contamination. There are two top mounts which are hard to see, but they should be fairly solid – a slight amount of give is OK but significant movement of the diff isn't good. There's a tie rod on each side of the diff casing, which bolts to the chassis and is rubber mounted to the diff. These rubber mounts can wear and cracks can develop around the point that the tie rod is bolted onto the chassis.

Under the bonnet

Firstly, check the bonnet. On the Elan, the bonnet is front 'hinged' on a pair of semi-circular rails, and is pulled up by springs. On the Plus 2, the bonnet is also front hinged, but pivots on a pair of bolts. Both bonnets should have soundproofing felt on their inside face. The Plus 2 has a steel bar running the length of the front, which carries the hinge bolts, and a second bar along its back edge carrying the two bonnet latches; both should be rust-free. In the engine bay, check for overall tidiness and lack of oil leaks. At this point, you can check which carburettors are fitted – Webers, Dellorto or Stromberg. Take off the oil filler cap and check that there's no white 'mayonnaise' – if there is, it may mean the head gasket is 'gone.'

Another very clean Plus 2 engine bay. Note the Weber carbs, brake servo and standard air box.

A late Elan Sprint engine bay. It sports the 'Big Valve' cam cover and Dellorto carburettors. Note the bonnet 'hinge' mechanism.

There are three types of cam cover used on the Elan and Plus 2. Up to around 1968, the cover had 'Lotus' cast in script on the top of each side of the cover. The next variant had 'LOTUS' written on the front crosspiece of the cover over the cam chain, and the final variant had 'LOTUS BIG VALVE' cast in to the front crosspiece. Not that all three types are interchangeable, and just because an engine has a 'Big Valve' cover, it's not a guarantee that the engine has the Sprint Spec big valve head. Post 1968, heads had a code letter, H, N or S, stamped on a raised round lug between the front plug and the cam chain tunnel. 'H' indicated a 10.5:1 high compression head, 'N' indicated High Compression big valve, and 'S' was used to indicate a big valve 9.5:1 compression ratio used on Federal cars.

Engine

With the engine off, carry out a visual inspection, then get the owner to start the engine. Listen closely for any heavy knocks from the unit indicating serious main or big end bearing wear, and lighter top end noise indicating out of adjustment or worn tappets. A rattle from the front of the twin-cam indicates timing chain wear. Use the stethoscope or long screwdriver to carefully check where any engine noises are coming from. The unit should settle down to a steady, even tickover fairly quickly. There should be little tappet noise from the engine; if the valve clearances need doing, the camshafts have to be removed and the tappets re-shimmed.

Once the engine has warmed up, and possibly after the test drive, ask the owner if you can use your compression tester on the engine. Take out all the

Federal Elans and Plus 2s had Stromberg carburettors with charge heating plumbing. This system of pipes used the heat from the manifold to heat the charge, which helped to reduce emissions. (Courtesy Scott Baron.)

spark plugs, which are nice and accessible on the Twin-Cam engines, although there may be a suppressor plate fitted above the plug well which will need to be removed. Spin the engine on the starter motor, with the throttle open for a few turns with the tester in each plug hole, and record the pressure readings. All the readings should be within 5-10psi of each other, and should be above about 120psi. Low overall readings indicate a tired engine which will potentially need a rebore or new rings and a top end overhaul. A low reading on one or more cylinders indicates a problem with that cylinder which, again, could be ring, bore or valve issues.

The most common carburettor fitment to the Elan and Plus 2 is a pair of twin-choke Webers.

The Lotus Twin-Cam engine is based on the Ford 1500 Kent block — this shows the pistons, camshafts, thermostat and exhaust ports.

Gearbox, clutch

Sitting in the car with the engine running, operate the clutch. It should be quiet and smooth, but a high-pitched squeal or a rumbling implies problems with the clutch release bearing, which is an engine-out job to fix. With the clutch down, try putting the car in gear; it should slip in and out easily. If the gears graunch, this could mean the clutch is worn and not disengaging fully. With the car in first gear, put your foot firmly on the brake and start to let out the clutch; the engine should slow down or stop as the clutch is released. If it doesn't, the clutch is slipping and needs replacement.

Soft top

The Elan's soft top should be reasonably draftproof and a good fit. Check the rear windows are clear, not discoloured or cracked, and that the hood fabric has no splits, cuts or tears. The hood mechanism should go up and down easily, and should

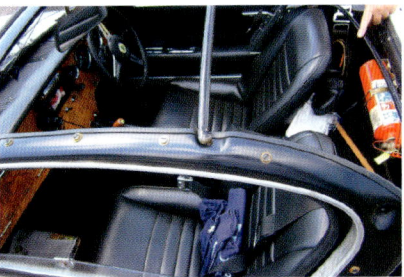

Series 1 and Series 2 Elan hoods used detachable transverse rails made from steel rods, and glass fibre cant rails around the doors. Putting the hood up or down meant the whole assembly needed to be disassembled.

be straight and rust-free. On the S1 and S2, it's removed completely from the car, along with the two rails that run over the side windows. On the S3 onwards, the hood and frame fold down into the well behind the seats.

From the Series 3, the frame hood was bolted to the body and the hood cover permanently attached to the frame. The entire hood and frame could be folded into the well behind the seats.

From the Series 3 onwards, the close-fitting and tightly-tensioned hood made the Elan virtually waterproof and draught-free. The good fit of the hood was helped by the fixed window surrounds.

Interior

Take a good look at the interior, starting with the door cards which should be free of any tears or rips. Check that the door mechanisms work properly and operate smoothly. Check that the electric windows work – they were never very fast, but they should go up and down smoothly at a constant speed.

Check the seat covers are in good condition, with no rips or collapsed foam, and that (on the Series 2 onwards) the seat adjuster mechanism works. Check the carpets; if they're damp then the car is leaking, so inspect the widow seals and door seals carefully. Rain can also penetrate the cabin via the seal around the pedal box. Check the car's dashboard for cracks, discolouration and lifting veneer, and make sure all the instruments and warning lights are working. The top of the dash should be crack-free, and see if the heater fan directs air onto the windscreen. In a Coupé or Plus 2, inspect the condition of the headlining, looking for rips or drooping.

The Plus 2 took the Elan's interior design to another level with a myriad of instruments and switches distributed over the veneered dashboard.

Door cards on the Plus 2 are simple but stylish. Note the British Leyland-sourced flush door latches and wide door aperture.

This Series 1 Elan interior shows the simple half-width dash and original alloy and wood rim steering wheel.

Controls 4 3 2 1

While sitting in the car, check for any slack or play in the gear change, the smooth operation of the clutch, choke and throttle cables, the feel of the brake pedal and the operation of the 'umbrella' style handbrake under the dash in front of the driver.

Do all the switches work properly? Check the lights, main beam, indicators, headlamp flasher, windows, fan and horn.

Headlights 4 3 2 1

The standard headlight mechanism on the Elan and Plus 2 is mechanically operated using a vacuum generated from the inlet manifold, with the front chassis crossmember acting as a vacuum reservoir to 'power' the system. There are two original systems. The earlier 'fail unsafe' system relies on the vacuum to hold the light pods up in their raised position, and when the vacuum is released, springs pull the pods down. It employs two vacuum cylinders, each one operating a headlamp pod.

The later 'failsafe' mechanism means the headlight pods are held up by springs and are pulled down by vacuum pressure. This system is easily identified by the use of a single vacuum cylinder operating on a rod, which links the two headlamp pods. With the engine running, both headlight pods should rise smoothly and reasonably quickly, and in-sync when the lights are turned on. If they don't, there are problems with the system. With the original system, the pods will stay down when the engine is off. With the failsafe system, the pods will rise slowly when the engine is off. If the pods raise up soon after the engine is turned off then there is a leak in the vacuum system. While this may just be a faulty joint in the plumbing, a failed component, or a corroded vacuum cylinder, it may indicate that the chassis crossmember is corroded and leaking.

The last of the Elans had a nicely appointed interior that was comfortable and snug. This Sprint has been fitted with a smaller aftermarket steering wheel.

The pop-up headlamps on the Elan and Plus 2 are a major styling feature.

Electrics 4 3 2 1

Walk round the car with the lights on and check that they're all working – including the indicators, brake lights and reversing lights – and that the lights are all reasonably bright, and the indicators flash at a reasonable rate.

Check the wiring loom where possible to identify any poor quality aftermarket wiring and dodgy connections. You need to look at the back of the dashboard above the driver's and passenger's footwells, in the front compartment and in and around the engine bay. Look out for:
• Neatly tied up wiring with no loose wires flapping about.

- Decent quality connectors – Lotus used bullet and spade connectors with properly soldered and crimped joins. Some aftermarket connectors are not as good; if present, inspect carefully.
- Any additional wires which are outside of the main loom clusters. What are they for and what sort of quality are they?
- The use of household flex, chocolate block screw connectors and bodges like wires twisted together and covered in insulation tape are real no-nos, bearing in mind the potentially disastrous results of an electrical fire.
- In general, any original wiring loom on an Elan or Plus 2 will be over four decades old, and will be in need of some attention. If the car has been re-wired, check for invoices and find out what's been done.

Starting and running

4 3 2 1

The car should start easily, but if it's been standing for a while, the mechanical fuel pump that's usually fitted will need to fill the carburettors, so it may need a number of turns before the engine fires (this is normal). The Twin-Cam usually won't need the choke if it's running on Webers or Dellortos – a couple of pumps of the accelerator pedal to squirt fuel into the inlet tract is usually enough to get the engine going, but the engine may need 'juggling' on the throttle while it warms up. Stromberg cars are a bit more civilised, and while they will need the choke, they should be reasonably well-behaved while warming up. Once the engine is warmed up, it should rev cleanly and crisply with no hesitation or stuttering, and there should be minimal tappet noise. The Twin-Cam engine, unless it's overtuned, has nice smooth power and torque curves, and there should be a smooth progression of power up to the red line. The engine should have a rev limiter fitted (as part of the rotor arm), but it's probably best not to test this yourself; ask the owner about it. There should be no pops and bangs in the exhaust on the overrun, which indicate the carburettors are not properly set up. At the end of the drive, the engine should stop as soon as the ignition is turned off, with no running on, which indicates problems with the points or that the cylinders are getting carboned up.

Test drive – passenger

4 3 2 1

When taking the car for a test drive, you should split it into two halves, firstly with you as a passenger so you can concentrate on looking and listening out for problems, then with you driving to assess how the car performs.

During the passenger part of the test drive, check for the following:

- Look carefully at the oil pressure from the gauge in the cabin; Miles Wilkins, author of *Lotus Twin-Cam Engine* (see bibliography), tells us that the Twin-Cam engine only needs 45psi to run reliably at 7000rpm, and normal running pressure should be 35-40psi, when hot. If the oil pressure is higher, quiz the owner to see if there's a high

A nice Plus 2S at a local show. Fitted with Lotus alloy wheels and with a great shine to the paintwork, it shows the Plus 2's unique lines.

capacity oil pump or modified pressure release valve fitted. Higher oil pressures will make the engine more prone to oil leaks.
- There should be an oil pressure warning light in the tachometer on early cars, and on the dash on later cars. Start the engine and see how quickly the light goes out; it should take around one second. Then turn the engine off and quickly turn the ignition back on; the light should take a couple of seconds to come back on as the oil pressure drops. This test shows if the oil pressure builds up quickly and drops slowly, indicating healthy engine bearings and oil pump. If the light isn't fitted, use the oil pressure gauge to carry out the test. A healthy engine will have a rapid rise in pressure and a slow drop, but the gauge is electrically triggered so, again, you will have to stall the engine or turn it off, then quickly turn the ignition back on.
- Listen for knocks, rattles or unusual noises while the car is accelerating, braking and cornering, and try to identify where they're coming from; is it the suspension, transmission, engine?
- A rumbling from the rear usually means a rear wheel bearing is on the way out.
- Check all the instruments are working properly.
- Look behind the car to see if there's any blue haze, indicating oil being burnt. If it appears while accelerating then the rings and/or the bores are worn. If it appears on deceleration, then the valve guides are tired. Persistent white smoke indicates head gasket failure, as does the engine temperature rising with high revs, then falling as the revs drop.
- Watch the oil pressure gauge. Fluctuating or falling oil pressure at high revs indicates worn mains and big end bearings, or possibly a faulty oil pump.
- If in an Elan Coupé or Plus 2, listen for wind noise from the door seals, as the car should be reasonably quiet inside.
- Check that the ventilation system works, with cold (ambient) air to the vents on the outside edge of the dash, and warm air to the screen and footwells.
- If the car is a convertible, try the car with the hood up first to check for excessive draughts, and the overall fit of the hood.

Test drive – driver

4 3 2 1

Now swap seats and drive the car yourself, but make sure you're insured to do so. Bear in mind that the Elan was an out and out sports car and the Plus was an accomplished and fast GT car, and both were blessed with excellent handling and roadholding. Even when compared with today's cars, both the Elan and Plus 2 should perform well.

Check the following as you drive the car:
- Does the throttle work smoothly, and is it light or notchy and stiff?
- Is the clutch reasonably light and smooth?
- How is the gear change? The Ford four-speed box had a reputation for a great change, with short travel and light action, while the Lotus five-speed had a less good reputation for gear change quality.

With the hood down and the cover clipped in place, this late DHC Series 4 Sprint looks neat and tidy.

43

- Is there good synchromesh on all gears?
- Does the car jump out of any gear under acceleration or on the overrun? If it does then a gearbox rebuild is needed.
- Are there any clonks or knocks while accelerating and decelerating? This could mean worn differential rubber mounts, or worn prop shaft universal joints.
- Does the car seem to be slow to accelerate initially when the throttle is opened, and does the engine rev or 'surge' when the throttle is opened or closed? This could be worn Rotoflex rubber joints in the driveshafts.

Performance:
- How does the car drive? Smooth and responsive or jerky and hesitant?
- Does it accelerate quickly and smoothly or is it hesitant and jerky, with flat spots?

Handling:
- Does it keep to a line in a corner, or does it need continual corrections?
- Does it track in a straight line on the road, or does it fall off the camber, or need constant correction to maintain a straight line?
- Is the steering light, precise and smooth or heavy, notchy and imprecise?

Brakes:
- Is the brake pedal firm or spongy?
- Do the brakes have 'feel' or are they wooden?
- Do the brakes slow the car quickly?
- Does the car pull up in a straight line?
- Do the rear brakes lock up under heavy braking, indicating a balance problem?

Finally:
- Do the speedometer and rev counter and all the minor gauges work?
- Is the seat comfortable or is the padding collapsed?

Evaluation criteria

Add up the total points scored in each section.

Score: 88 = excellent, possibly concours; 66 = good; 44 = average; 22 = poor. Excellent cars should be close to concours standard, with only a few minor faults. Good cars should be reliable runners, with few faults; hopefully nothing that needs immediate attention, but the assessment should highlight any that do. Average cars will have a number of problems, both minor and major, and will need a careful assessment of the problems to satisfy the potential buyer, if they're prepared to fix them. Poor cars will potentially need a full restoration.

Despite the above scores, if the chassis is showing signs of significant rust then it needs to be repaired or replaced. In virtually every case, the body will need to come off for any repairs to be done properly, and when the body is off it's pretty much a certainty that more rust will be discovered in the chassis.

Pistachio green over white was a typically '70s colour combination offered by Lotus. While it sounds garish, it actually works really well, as shown by this Sprint.

10 Auctions
– sold! Another way to buy your dream

Auction pros and cons
Auctions give owners a reliable and secure way of selling their cars, and they give buyers the chance to buy with minimal hassle. The price achieved is often lower than the 'market' value, and this gives the buyers a potential bargain, but the cars are usually sold as-seen, and there is very little comeback, unless the car has been wrongly described. An auction may also be used to dispose of a troublesome car or a car which needs more work than a dealer or owner is prepared to put into it.

Which auction?
It's pretty unlikely that a classic car like an Elan or Plus 2 will appear in a 'normal' trade-oriented auction, but it's not impossible, and you might pick up a bargain if one is entered into your local modern vehicle event. However, you are much more likely to find an Elan or Plus 2 at a specialist classic vehicle auction. The classic vehicle press usually carries adverts for these auctions, and will often have a list of entries.

Catalogue, entry fee and payment details
The auction catalogue acts as your ticket into the auction and viewing days, and will give limited data on all of the auction entries (it may not cover late or last-minute entries). It should also give details of how to pay – an auction will not release a car until it's been paid for with verified funds – and of the buyer's premium, storage costs and any charges for credit card usage. Find out in advance what the procedure is for registering, sorting out bank details or other payment methods, getting your bid paddle or number, what time the auction starts and when the car you're interested in will be on the rostrum. Finally, find out if you have to take the car away after the auction or if it can be stored until you can pick it up (which will incur additional costs).

Buyer's premium
It's important to remember that the price the car is 'hammered down' to is not the price you'll have to pay. On top of the hammer price, there will be a 'buyer's fee,' which will be a percentage of the hammer price. It's usual for there to be a local tax, such as VAT, to pay on the buyer's fee as well, and you should check to see if there's any additional tax added to the hammer price. Take your time to work out what these 'extras' add to the price, and use the information to work out what your maximum bid can be.

Viewing
There are limited viewing opportunities at an auction. Some will have viewing days where you can have a good poke around, some may only allow you to see the car on the day of the auction. Either way, your access to the car will be limited to opening doors and lids. You may get auction staff to start the car up for you, but you won't be allowed to jack the car up, take off wheels and do the sort of in-depth check outlined in chapter 9. However, you may be able to carry out most of the initial assessment, as described in chapter 7. The auction staff should be able to let you see any documentation that comes with the car, but you will not be able to take the car for a test drive, and the staff will have little or no knowledge of the individual car.

Bidding

At the auction itself, each car will only be on the rostrum for a short time, so make sure you know when your car is due to appear. You'll need to be quick and assertive with your bids, making it clear to the auctioneer that you're bidding. If the bidding goes above your limit, make it clear you're stopping bidding with a definite shake of the head. If you're successful, the auctioneer will make a note of your paddle number, and from then on you're the owner, and you're responsible for the vehicle. If the reserve on the car was not met, it may be possible to negotiate a sale with the vendor through the auction house.

Successful bid

If you win the auction, you will hopefully have worked out beforehand how you're going to pay and get the car home. This could be driving it, using a trailer which you've bought with you, or arranging for a company to transport it home for you.

If you're driving it home, it must be taxed and insured. While some insurance companies sell limited cover insurance on-site, it's usually more cost effective to make arrangements with your own insurance company to activate cover over the phone.

eBay and other online auction sites

eBay and other online auction sites could get you a car at a bargain price, although you'd be foolish to buy a car without seeing it and examining it.

Be aware that some cars offered for sale on eBay may be 'ghost' cars, which don't actually exist. Scammers will take pictures and descriptions from other websites and build an eBay entry using them, which will invariably be at a price that's well below the market rate. One way to spot these is to copy and paste the text or a picture into a search engine to see if it pops up anywhere else on the web. If it does, it's likely to be a scam. If the vendor is evasive or has lots of excuses as to why you can't view the car then, again, that's a sure sign of a scam.

Auctioneers

The auction market can be divided in two, with National or international companies running prestigious auctions at various sites and, in the UK and elsewhere, smaller local companies who will hold classic car auctions a few times each year. Internationals include:

    Barrett-Jackson *barrett-jackson.com*
    Bonhams *bonhams.com*
    British Car Auctions (BCA)
        bca-europe.com or
        british-car-auctions.co.uk
    Cheffins *cheffins.co.uk*
    Christies *christies.com*
    Coys *coys.co.uk*
    eBay *eBay.com*
    H&H Classics *handh.co.uk*
    RM *RMauctions.com*
    Shannons *shannons.com.au*
    Silver *silverauctions.com*
    Silverstone Auctions
        silverstoneauctions.com

Smaller local auction houses include:
    Anglia Car Auctions in Norfolk *angliacarauctions.co.uk*
    Brightwells in Herefordshire *brightwells.com*
    Essex Classic Car Auctions in Essex *ecca.club*
    Mathewsons Classic Car Auctions in North Yorkshire *mathewsons.co.uk*
    Morris Leslie in Perth *morrisleslie.com*
    South Western Vehicle Auctions in Dorset *swva.co.uk*

11 Paperwork
– correct documentation is essential!

The paper trail
Every car should have some sort of paper trail that will allow you to establish its provenance. Typical UK documentation is discussed below. Outside of the UK, local rules will apply, so make sure you familiarise yourself with them.

Registration documents
In the UK, every vehicle used on the road must be registered. The official document to record the registration is called a V5C. It's a four-page A4 document which records the vehicle details and ownership details, and is used to manage the transfer of a vehicle when it's sold. Note that in the UK, the V5C records the 'registered keeper,' and this may not be the actual owner of the car, nor is the V5C proof of ownership.

Other countries have different systems, so you need to familiarise yourself with whatever system is in operation locally.

Correct documentation is important. Take time to inspect it, and make sure everything is in order.

Roadworthiness certificate
In the UK, after April 2018, all Elans and Plus 2s are over 40 years old, so they won't need an MoT test to be used on the road. However, if the car was on the road between 2005 and 2018, the car's MoT history should still be available from the DVLA at www.gov.uk/check-mot-history. The site will give you the milage at the test, and any failures and advisories. Other countries may have local test regimes for their cars to ensure roadworthiness – you should check the details. Some countries have separate emissions and noise tests, so ask to see details if the car needs to comply. Note that compliance with a test will only ensure the car complied on the date of the test, and you should satisfy yourself that the car is roadworthy.

Road licence or tax
In the UK, all Elans and Plus 2s are zero-rated for road tax, so while you do have to have the car taxed, it doesn't cost anything. Note that when you buy a car, the tax immediately lapses, so you need to re-tax it before you drive it on the road. Instructions on how to do this online or at a Post Office are on the V5C.

Buying an imported car in the UK
If you're buying a car in the UK which has been imported, then you need to follow a process to get it registered before you can use it on the road. The process does

47

change from time to time, but at the time of publication there are four steps you need to take before you can drive the car on the road. These are:
• Tell HM Revenue and Customs that the vehicle has arrived in the UK.
• Pay the VAT and Duty due.
• Get vehicle approval to show that it meets safety and environmental standards.
• Register and tax the vehicle.
If the car has a NOVA (Notification of Vehicle Arrival) certificate, this indicates that the HMRC have been notified and the tax and duty are paid. DVLA will issue you with a 'used vehicle import pack' on request from www.gov.uk. This will guide you through the process, but you'll have to provide evidence of the age of the car, an MOT test if applicable (all Elans and Plus 2s will be MOT exempt from 2018 when a new regime comes in) and proof that all import taxes have been paid. The proof of age can be taken from the original registration document from the country the car was imported from, if it has that information on it (most USA titles do), or from a dating certificate from an authorised club; in the Elan and Plus 2's case this is Club Lotus or a Lotus Heritage Certificate. An Elan or Plus 2 will not need an MOT test certificate, and the NOVA certificate tells the DVLA that all duty and VAT has been paid. Full current details of the process are summarised on the Federation of British Historic Vehicle Clubs website (www.FBHVC.co.uk) and on the 'driving and transport' section of the UK Government portal (www.gov.uk).

Certificate of authenticity/heritage certificate
Lotus can issue an official 'Certificate of Provenance' for any Lotus produced from 1957 onwards. The Certificate includes the full VIN, model and variant, the original engine and gearbox serial numbers, body and trim colours, options fitted, build date, and the original dealer or distributor the car was dispatched to. Contact Andy Graham in Lotus Archives at Archive@lotuscars.com or telephone +44 1603 732178 for further details and costs.

Official valuation
Some insurance companies will offer 'Agreed Valuations' for classic cars. Getting a valuation can be as simple as sending the Insurer some pictures of the car, or it may involve having a professional assessment of the car by a recognised expert. The valuation will not take into account every market fluctuation, so it may not reflect the market value of the car after it's agreed. Either way, the valuation also reflects the time and effort it would take for the owner to replace the car, so it may well be higher than the current market value. It also tends to cover the cost of buying a replacement from a dealer, so it will include a premium to cover the dealer's costs. It can act as a starting point for negotiation if you're interested in buying the car, but it's not a 'list price.'

Service and restoration history
Most cars should have some sort of service history, ranging from a selection of receipts for parts and notes written by the owner, to a full-blown professional invoice for regular servicing by marque specialists. What the information should give is a picture of the previous ownership of the car, and items such as old MOT certificates and receipts for service item such as oil, filters etc all add to the picture.
    If the car has had a full restoration, it's not unreasonable to have supporting invoices and photos of the work undertaken.

12 What's it worth?
– let your head rule your heart

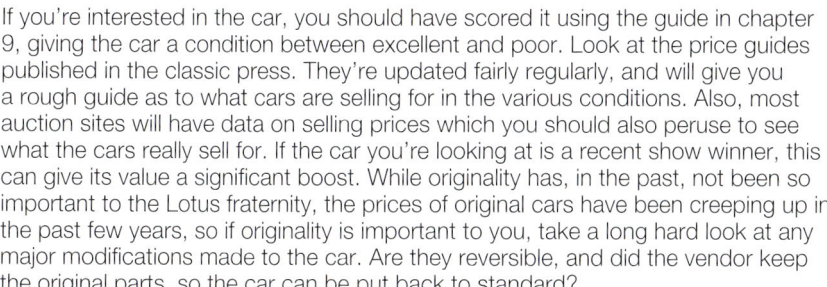

Condition
If you're interested in the car, you should have scored it using the guide in chapter 9, giving the car a condition between excellent and poor. Look at the price guides published in the classic press. They're updated fairly regularly, and will give you a rough guide as to what cars are selling for in the various conditions. Also, most auction sites will have data on selling prices which you should also peruse to see what the cars really sell for. If the car you're looking at is a recent show winner, this can give its value a significant boost. While originality has, in the past, not been so important to the Lotus fraternity, the prices of original cars have been creeping up in the past few years, so if originality is important to you, take a long hard look at any major modifications made to the car. Are they reversible, and did the vendor keep the original parts, so the car can be put back to standard?

If you're buying from a dealer, they'll have an added premium to cover their overheads and any warranty. Buying from an auction will include a buyer's premium.

Extras and modifications
Major modifications are a bit of a double-edged sword. Some will add value, some may detract value, and some will put the car into a different market sector. Engine and suspension tuning is a common Lotus owner pastime, and the Twin-Cam unit in particular has considerable tuning potential. However, an over-tuned engine can be a pain to use on the road or in town. In addition, some track-oriented suspension modifications, such as stiffer dampers and higher-rated springs, can ruin the car's good road manners and comfortable ride, for the sake of

This Lotus Elan Sprint's Big Valve engine has been fitted with fuel-injection to boost performance and tractability.

marginally improved handling on a smooth circuit. Thinner rear springs can be fitted to allow the fitment of wider tyres and wheels. Electronic ignition is a useful and practical modification, which should reduce maintenance and increase reliability. Removing the standard air box and replacing it with aftermarket air filters may increase performance, but it will also increase induction noise and may be a fire risk – the carbs sit just above the distributor, and fuel and sparks outside of the engine don't mix.

Replacing the Rotoflex-equipped standard rear driveshafts with CV or universal joint units is common, especially as the price of good quality Rotoflexes keeps on rising. While you lose some cushioning from the drivetrain, fitting solid driveshafts (or Spyder ones, with one UJ and one Rotoflex) makes sense, and cuts down on maintenance. There are bolt-on kits available to replace the vacuum headlamp mechanism with an electric motor.

While the original chassis had minimal corrosion protection, replacement Lotus units are now galvanised, giving great resistance to corrosion, but with a non-standard finish. Spyder Cars (see chapter 17 for contact details) makes replacement space frame chassis which are made from square section tube, and are slightly heavier, more rigid and less prone to rusting than the Lotus original. They also have provision for revised rear suspension, and are generally considered to be a good alternative to the Lotus item.

There have been a number of conversions of Type 36 Coupés into dhc format – a relatively simple operation, bearing in mind that the cars share the same bodyshell and parts are readily available, but it may impact the car's value. Plus 2s were never supplied from the factory as convertibles, but there have been a couple of dealers offering conversions, and these do come up on the market from time to time.

After the Elan ceased production in 1973, there have been at least two attempts to re-introduce them. The Christopher Neil Sprint was a kit of parts to build up a new Elan, which was marketed during the late 1970s, and was virtually identical to the original Sprint. The Evante, also based on the Sprint, was produced in the 1980s by Lotus specialist Vegantune, and featured a modified bodyshell with wide arches and a boot lid 'lip' spoiler, and Vegantune's take on the Twin-Cam engine, with their belt-driven DOHC unit.

The replacement of the engine with a modern unit, such as a Ford Zetec, Duratec or Vauxhall 'Red Top,' will move the car out of the classic market and into the modified market. Values of such modified cars can only be defined on a one-off basis, so are really out of the scope of this guide.

Striking a deal

When it comes to agreeing a price, your assessment of the car and its ownership history should have exposed any faults, and the cost of rectification should be factored into any reduction you can negotiate. Most owners will be enthusiasts, and will have a good idea of the car's value.

The Plus 2 was never offered as a soft top by the factory, but various third parties did offer kits. The car's design lends itself to the conversion, as shown by this neat example.

The Vegantune Evante was a development of the Elan. Now rare, they're usually powered by Vegantune's own take on the Lotus Twin-Cam engine. Note the modified Elan bodywork with flared wheelarches and nose spoiler.

Replacing the Lotus Twin-Cam engine with a modern Ford unit is popular. While most people fit Zetec units, this Elan has been re-engined with a Duratec unit, which has the inlet and exhaust sides reversed when compared to the original Twin-Cam or Zetec.

13 Do you really want to restore?
– it'll take longer and cost more than you think

Buying a restoration project may be a way of getting into Elan or Plus 2 ownership at a low initial cost, but be aware of what you're getting into. The actual costs of a professional restoration will almost always exceed the value of the finished car. However, if you're mechanically able, prepared to learn how to restore glass fibre bodywork, intend to do most of the work yourself, and don't charge for your time, there's a possibility that you can complete a restoration and have a car that's worth more than your outlay. Restoring a car as a hobby is perfectly viable, and you have

Barn or garage finds do still come to light. The author bought this car in 2011 as a restoration project.

the satisfaction of doing all the work yourself and knowing that the car has been restored properly. However, a full restoration will take at least twice as long and cost twice as much as your initial estimates, so if you want to buy a car in the spring to run through the summer, don't get a restoration project! A final consideration is space. As you dismantle the car, you will need at least as much floor space or racking space again as the car takes up on its own, to store the bits you've taken off. Manage the space carefully, so you don't lose anything.

As this guide was being written in 2018, there were still a small but steady number of 'barn find' or 'restoration project' Elans and Plus 2s trickling onto the market at prices significantly below those of running cars. If you decide to buy such a car, you need to ask two questions; why was the car taken off the road in the first place, and is the car complete and in one piece?

Working cars in good condition, with nothing wrong with them, are rarely put into barns or abandoned. It's likely that they have some mechanical event which was not worth fixing at the time, ranging from some catastrophic failure to lots of little issues that meant the car would not pass its next MoT test. Either way, the car will need more than just simple recommissioning to get it into roadworthy condition. Also, bear in mind that the car would have been used, and was probably a typical old sports car when it was stored, so it will also need a certain amount of ancillary work to the cosmetics and non-vital parts to bring it back into good condition. In the case of the Plus 2, prices have been low over the past couple of decades, and many cars have had their engines removed for use in historic racing, or other more valuable cars such as Elans, Lotus Cortinas or Escort Twin-Cams. A replacement Twin-Cam engine is not cheap, although it's possible to build one up from spare parts. Cars without engines are the cheapest way into Plus 2 ownership, and it's relatively easy and cheap to slot a Ford Zetec engine in. Getting hold of a Twin-Cam engine is more expensive, but it's still a viable way of getting an enginless Plus 2 on the road.

If the car is still in one piece, and hasn't been partially or totally stripped down, then you're in a position to assess the car for completeness and condition. If you're going to take on a restoration, it's best to make the assumption that you'll be replacing all wearing parts from the engine, gearbox, rolling chassis and bodyshell, as well as doing a complete respray. Rolling chassis parts would include suspension bushes, swivels, trunnions, springs and dampers, trackrod ends and anything else that moves or rotates, and possibly the chassis. The engine may need its crank reground and a rebore, as well as a cylinder head overhaul. It will need, as a minimum, new bearings, piston rings, valve guides and seals, a new timing chain, a new water pump for the twin-cam and all-new auxiliary belts. The carburettor and the electrical system will need to be overhauled. The interior might need a retrim, with new or repaired carpets, seat covers, door cards, dashboard, dash top, centre console and headlining, and the instruments may need refurbishing. If the car has been left in a hot and dry state then all the door and window rubbers may need replacing. The wheels will need new tyres and a repaint. The elephant in the room is the bodywork. Will it need a respray or can the original finish be saved, and are there any old repairs which need to be redone?

This Plus 2 shows the result of a stalled restoration, with semi-stripped paintwork and many components removed.

This Plus 2 has had only two owners. It's complete, but has a rotten chassis and major body issues – it's an excellent basis for a project.

A car that's been stripped down to its component parts has one major issue; which parts are missing? Also, if it's your first restoration of an Elan or Plus 2, you have the unenviable task of working out what all the bits in those boxes actually are. Do they belong to the car? If they do, how do they fit? Buying such a car is a brave thing to do and the price should reflect that!

If you're going to take on a restoration, here are a few tips from the author's experiences. The main thing is to be methodical and finish off one job before starting another. When you start to strip the car down, keep as many assemblies as big as possible, and only break them down to their component parts when you start to refurbish them. Finally, bag and tag everything you take off the car.

- Break the job up into manageable chunks and do one thing at a time. I would suggest that you split the job into three main tasks: Chassis and Suspension; Engine and Transmission; and Body.
- Strip down and assess the chassis, and replace it or repair it.
- Refurbish the front and rear suspension, then fit to the chassis. This gives you a rolling chassis in as-new condition.
- Strip down and rebuild the engine.
- Strip down and rebuild the gearbox.
- Fit the engine and gearbox to the chassis.
- Do all the bodyshell repairs, and refit to the rolling chassis.
- Respray the body, if needed.
- Refurbish and refit the interior trim, wiring loom, rubbers etc.
- At the end of the process, you'll have a car that you can be proud of and you will have learned a lot about the Elan or Plus 2, and about how to restore cars in general.

14 Paint problems
– bad complexion, including dimples, pimples and bubbles

While the Elan's glass fibre body means there are no rust problems, this doesn't mean there are no problems with the paint on the cars. Glass fibre is not as stable as steel, which means that paintwork repairs and full resprays need a lot more preparation than on steel. Any paintwork on an Elan or Plus 2 will take longer to do, and hence will cost more, than the equivalent work on a steel bodied car. As well as the gel coat cracking and blistering described in chapter 9, the following are general issues with paintwork.

Orange peel
This appears as an uneven paint surface, similar in appearance to the skin of an orange. It's caused by the failure of the atomised paint droplets to flow into each other when they hit the surface of the panel. If the paint layer is thick enough, it's possible to rub out the effect using fine wet and dry sandpaper and rubbing compound, but in severe cases a respray would be needed.

Orange peel.

Cracking
Cracking in the paint layer is likely to be caused by too thick a layer of paint being applied, incorrect mixing of the paint before spraying, or a reaction with an existing paint layer. If the damage is limited to the paint, it can be repaired by rubbing down and respraying the affected area. If the paint is cracked due to damage to the underlying gel coat or glass fibre, then all the paint will have to be removed, the cracks in the gel coat or glass fibre ground out and repaired properly, and the whole area then resprayed.

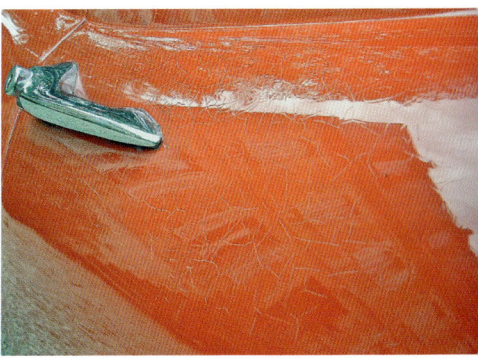

Cracking and crazing.

Crazing
Crazing is when the paint takes on a load of small cracks, and is usually caused by the same issues as cracking. Repairs are the same.

Blistering and micro blistering
The appearance of small or large blisters (also referred to in the boat industry as osmosis) is usually caused by water in the paint, or the glass fibre being damp, when the car was sprayed. Caused by liquid being trapped between the glass

53

fibre and the gel coat or the paint layer, blistering will sometimes appear if the car has been kept in a damp environment or under a non-breathing car cover, and may disappear once the car is in a warmer dry place. The only way to prevent blistering is to keep the car in a dry environment, and to make sure the bodyshell is properly dried out before spraying.

Fading

When the Elan and Plus 2 were built, Lotus initially used cellulose paint, then moved on to acrylic types. Both of these paints, especially in colours up at the red end of the spectrum, could react to light, causing the paint to fade. Faded paint may be recovered using rubbing compound to remove the layer of damaged paint and, if successful, the paint should be protected with a good quality wax polish. Bad cases of fading may only be fixed with a respray.

Modern paints are a lot more stable, and fading should not be an issue if the car has been resprayed using two-pack or the current water-based paint.

Peeling

Older metallic paints with a top layer of lacquer can be prone to the lacquer failing and peeling off. Poorly applied paint or poor preparation may also cause peeling. The only solution is to strip the paint back and respray.

An extreme example of paint blistering on a Plus 2. The integrity of the paint is compromised, and removal and a respray is the only option.

Typical microblistering. While this is a Series 1 Europa. Elans and Plus 2s can have the same problem.

Dimples/fish eyes

Dimples or 'fish eyes' appear as imperfections in the paint layer, and are caused by surface contamination, most often due to the presence of silicon-based polish. Removing the paint, cleaning the subsurface and respraying is the only cure.

Pinstripes

When the Elan Sprint was produced with side stripes, the stripes were stick-on decals supplied to Lotus in the right width. The decals were lightproof, so they were not lacquered over on the cars.

15 Problems due to lack of use
– just like their owners, Elans need exercise!

Despite their corrosion-free body, the Elan and Plus 2 will deteriorate if not used regularly. Take them on a decent run at least once a week to make sure everything that turns and burns is properly warmed up and exercised.

An extreme example of decay due to lack of use. The car will require a complete rebuild.

Seized components: Any moving component can seize up through lack of use. In the engine, moisture can cause the piston rings to stick to the wall of the bores, and corrosion can cause excessive wear, or break the piston rings, resulting in loss of compression and excessive oil consumption. The clutch plate can corrode onto the flywheel, resulting in no clutch and a damaged clutch plate when it's freed. The pistons in the brake calipers, and the handbrake cable and mechanism, can sieze.

Fuel system: The carburettors will suffer if not used. If the car is left standing for a long time, all the fuel remaining in the carbs will evaporate, leaving behind a gummy deposit. This will harden over time, and the longer it's left, the less likely it is that a new shot of fuel will clear it.

Fluids: Old Engine oil can become acidic over time and cause damage to bearings. If the engine is started then turned off before it's warmed up, water can contaminate the oil, casuing corrosion. The cooling water in the engine should be properly mixed with anti-freeze to inhibit corrosion. Brake fluid is hygroscopic, which means it can absorb water from the atmosphere. Once water is in the system, it will corrode the pistons in calipers, master, slave, and brake cylinders, and corrode steel brake lines from the inside. Silicone brake fluid isn't hygroscopic, but it's still a good idea to change the fluid in the brake and clutch systems every couple of years.

Tyres: Tyres can develop flat spots which will cause vibration while driving. If they're allowed to go flat, then left with the weight of the car on them, permanent damage will occur. Tyres should be replaced when they're eight to ten years old (see chapter 9 for details on how to date a tyre).

Shock absorbers or dampers: Shock absorbers deteriorate if the car isn't used. Oil reservoir seals can harden and stop working properly, leading to leaks.

Rubber and plastic components: Rubber and plastic components, such as windscreen wipers, gaiters, window seals, front and rear screen rubbers, suspension bushes and cooling hoses, will harden and crack with time.

Electrics: Batteries will be ruined if they're fully discharged. Connectors in the loom can corrode and, with the need for earthing circuits due to the glass fibre bodyshell, there are many more connectors to corrode than on a steel-bodied car. The contacts inside the switches can corrode through lack of use, especially if the car is left in a hot or humid environment, or if the factory lube dries out.

Exhaust system: Any exhaust system has a hard life and, on cars that see little use, condensation and combustion deposits form a corrosive mix.

16 The Community

– key people, organisations and companies in the Elan world

Introduction
There are a wide range of sources for information on the Elan and Plus 2, including books, clubs, web forums and marque specialists. In the UK, Club Lotus and the Lotus Drivers Club cater for the Elan and Plus 2, and both clubs hold regular local meetings and national events.

Web resources
lotuselan.net is the go-to source for expertise on the Elan and Plus 2. With various threads addressing the Elan, Plus 2, modifications, and mechanical components, it's a rich source of information about the cars and parts for sale, and it's building an archive of Elan-related articles. It's friendly as well, with a worldwide presence and plenty of members in the UK, USA and Europe.

thelotusforums.com, as the name suggests, supports a number of forums about all Lotus cars, including an Elan and Plus 2 thread.

Clubs
UK Clubs:
Club Lotus (clublotus.co.uk)
Lotus Drivers Club (lotusdriversclub.org.uk)
USA Clubs:
Golden Gate Lotus Club (gglotus.org)
LOONY – Lotus owners of New York (lotusowners.com)

Suppliers
The following suppliers all stock various levels of Elan and Plus 2 spares. They have either been used by the author or they have a good reputation:
- Kelvedon Lotus, Bourne Road, Spalding, Lincolnshire, PE11 3ND, Tel: +44 (0)1775 725 457, kelsport.net
- Mick Miller Classic Lotus, Carlton Cross, Main Road, Lelsale, Suffolk, IP17 2NL, +44 1728 603307, mickmillerlotus.com

Club Lotus runs a number of events throughout the year, where lots of Lotus owners and their cars congregate. This is the scene at Castle Combe on a track day.

Brands Hatch race circuit was a popular venue for a Club Lotus event in 2014. Lots of Lotuses, and lots of track action for their owners. Here, a nice Plus 2 is surrounded by other Lotuses.

Still at Brands Hatch, 2014, and a lovely Series 4 Elan Coupé basks in the sunshine, surrounded by modern and classic Lotuses.

- Paul Matty Sportscars, 12 Old Birmingham Road, Bromsgrove, Worcs, B60 1DE, +44 (0)1527 835656, paulmattysportscars.co.uk
- SJ Sportscars, Lotus House, Marsh End, Lords Meadow Industrial Estate, Crediton, Devon EX17 1DN, +44(0)1363 777790, sjsportscars.com
- Spydercars Ltd, 136 Station Road Industrial Estate, Whittlesey, Peterborough, Cambs, PE7 2EY, Tel +44 (0)1733 203986, spydercars.co.uk
- Tony Thompson Racing (TTR), Kings Road, Melton Mowbray LE13 1QF, Tel +44 (0)1664 566777, tonythompsonracing.co.uk

The following suppliers provide spares for the Lotus Twin-Cam engines:
- Burton Power, 617-631 Eastern Ave, Ilford, Essex IG2 6PN, Tel +44(0)20 8518 9136, burtonpower.com
- QED Motor Sports Ltd, 4 Soar Road, Quorn, Leics, LE12 8BN, +44 (0)1509 416317, qedmotorsport.co.uk

Useful books

Lotus still produces workshop manuals and parts books, and there are a number of books, both in and out of print, which cover the Elan and Plus 2.
- *Lotus Elan Gold Portfolio*, R. M. Clarke, Brooklands Books, ISBN 1 85520 5513. A collection of road tests and articles on the Elan and Plus 2.
- *Lotus Elan – The Complete Story*, Matthew Vale, The Crowood Press, ISBN 9781 84797 510 2. A history of the Elan, Plus 2 and the M100 Elan.
- *Lotus Elan*, Mike Taylor, The Crowwod Press, ISBN 1 85523 349 4. Covers the history of the Elan and Plus 2, up to the introduction of the then-new M100 Elan.
- *The Original Lotus Elan*, Robinshaw and Ross. Originally published by Motor Racing Publications with ISBN 0 947981 32 2, and reprinted by Brooklands Books with ISBN 978 1783180004. This well-researched book gives essential data and guidance on the Elan.
- *Authentic Lotus Elan and Plus 2*, Robinshaw and Ross, Motor Racing Publications. ISBN 0 947981 95 0. This is an extension of Robinshaw and Ross's 'Original Lotus Elan,' which has been revised to cover the Plus 2.
- *The Rebuilding of a Lotus Elan – Addendum Engineering Workshop Manual*, Brian Buckland, Elanman Ltd, ISBN 978-0-9552849-0-8. A comprehensive guide to restoring the Lotus Elan (with lots of information relevant to the Plus 2). An invaluable resource for the Elan restorer, based on years of experience of maintaining and restoring Elans.
- *Lotus Elan Restoration Guide*, Gordon Lund, Brooklands Books, ISBN 9781855209466. A guide to the restoration of an Elan and Plus 2.
- *Lotus: The Elan, Cortina and Europa*, Richard Newton and Raymond Psulkowski, Tab Books Inc, ISBN0-8306-2106-07. Good coverage of the Elan and Plus 2, alongside the Europa and Lotus Cortina.
- *Lotus: the Elite, Elan Europa by Chris Harvey,* Haynes, ISBN 0 902280 85 6. A useful book on the Elan and Plus 2, along with the Europa and Type 14 Elite.
- *Lotus Elan and Europa: A Collector's Guide*, John Bolster, ISBN 0-900594-48-3, Motor Racing Publications. A good description of the Elan, Plus 2 and Europa.
- *Lotus Twin-Cam Engine*, Miles Wilkins, re-published by Brooklands Books, ISBN 9781855209688. A recent reprint of the definitive guide to the design, development, rebuilding and maintaining the Lotus Twin-Cam engine.

17 Vital statistics
– essential data at your fingertips

Dimensions

	Elan	Plus 2
Length	145.25in / 3690cm	168.75in / 428.6cm
Height	45in / 1140cm	47in / 119.3cm
Width	56in / 1420cm	66.25in / 168.2cm
Wheelbase	84in / 2130cm	96in / 243.8cm
Weight	1288lb / 584.2kg	1904lb / 863kg
Fuel capacity	10gal / 45.45l	13gal / 59l
Wheels and tyres	145x13 (S4 155x13)	165x13

Production numbers
A lot of the original Lotus production records were lost when their archive was flooded, but looking at various sources (notably Robinshaw and Ross's books – see bibliography) there were between 8676 and 9153 Elans produced, along with between 4526 and 5228 Plus 2s, in total.

Engine details

	Twin-Cam	SE spec	Big Valve Sprint
Type	Cast Iron block, alloy cylinder head	Cast Iron block, alloy cylinder head	Cast Iron block, alloy cylinder head
Bore and stroke	82.55mm x 72.75mm	82.55mm x 72.75mm	82.55mm x 72.75mm
Capacity	1558cc	1558cc	1558cc
Valve gear	Double overhead cams operating two valves per cylinder	Double overhead cams operating two valves per cylinder	Double overhead cams operating two valves per cylinder (Big Valve head)
Compression ratio	9.5:1	9.5:1	10.3:1
Power	105bhp @ 6000rpm	115bhp @ 6000rpm	126bhp @ 6500rpm
Torque	103ft lb @ 4500rpm	108ft lb @ 4000rpm	113ft lb @ 5500rpm
Carburettor	Twin Weber 40 DCOE	Twin Weber 40 DCOE	Twin Dellorto 40 DHLA

Note that Federal versions of the Twin-Cam were fitted with two Stromberg 175 CV carburettors and, in Sprint specification, produced 113bhp @ 6500rpm and 104ft lbs @ 4500rpm.

Lotus type numbers

Series 1 and 2 Elans were assigned the Lotus model designation Type 26, all the Elan Coupés were Type 36, and the Series 3, 4 and Sprint Elans were Type 45. All the Plus 2 models – the Plus 2, Plus 2S, Plus 2S 130 and the Plus 2 S 130/5 – were Type 50.

Chassis/VIN

Up to the end of 1969, the Elan and Plus 2's VIN was of the format XX/0001, where 'XX' is the Lotus Type number, and '0001' is the unit number. According to various sources, Elan Series 1 cars (Type 26) started at 26/0001 running to 26/3900, Series 2 cars (still Type 26) ran from 26/3901 to 26/5798, Coupés (Type 36) started at 36/4510 to 36/9824 at December 1969. The Type 45 Series 3 dhc (Type 45) ran from 45/45/5701, and the Series 4 fhc started at 45/7895, the sequence ending at 45/9823, when the new numbering system was adopted. From January 1970, Lotus changed their numbering system to conform to international standards.

Plus 2 (Type 50) ran from 50/0001 to 50/1592, when the Plus 2S was introduced at 50/1593, and production ran to 50/2536 when the numbering system changed.

The new system was of the form: 7001.011234A, where 7001 represents the year (1970) and Month (01 – January), 01 is the production batch (sometimes omitted), 1234 is the unit number, and 'A' is the model code – in the Elan and Plus 2's case this should be 'A' to 'N' (but not including 'I'). The model assignment is:

Code	Model	Type	Market
A	Elan Standard	Coupé	Great Britain and Northern Ireland
B	Elan Standard	Coupé	Export
C	Elan Standard	Convertible	Great Britain and Northern Ireland
D	Elan Standard	Convertible	Export
E	Elan SE	Coupé	Great Britain and Northern Ireland
F	Elan SE	Coupé	Export
G	Elan SE	Convertible	Great Britain and Northern Ireland
H	Elan SE	Convertible	Export
J	Elan Federal	Coupé	Export
K	Elan Federal	Convertible	Export
L	Plus 2S	Coupé	Great Britain and Northern Ireland
M	Plus 2S	Coupé	Export
N	Plus 2S	Coupé	Export

Ending with a rarity: this is the Elan-based Ian Walker Racing Coupé that successfully competed in the 1960s. Now fully restored, it's an interesting adjunct to the history of the Elan.

Also from Veloce:

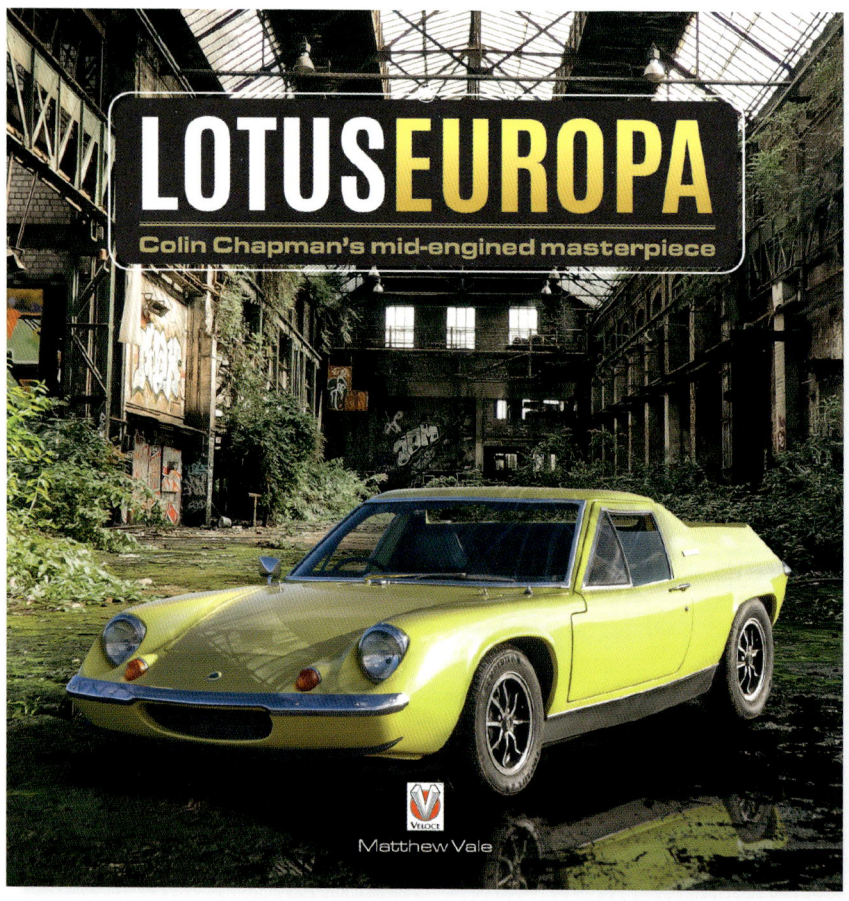

ISBN: 978-1-787112-84-1
Hardback • 25x25cm • 160 pages • 175 pictures

Explores the design development and production of the Lotus Europa, Lotus' first mid-engined road car. It covers the Renault-powered Series 1 and 2 cars, the Lotus Twin-Cam-engined versions, and the Type 47 racing models.

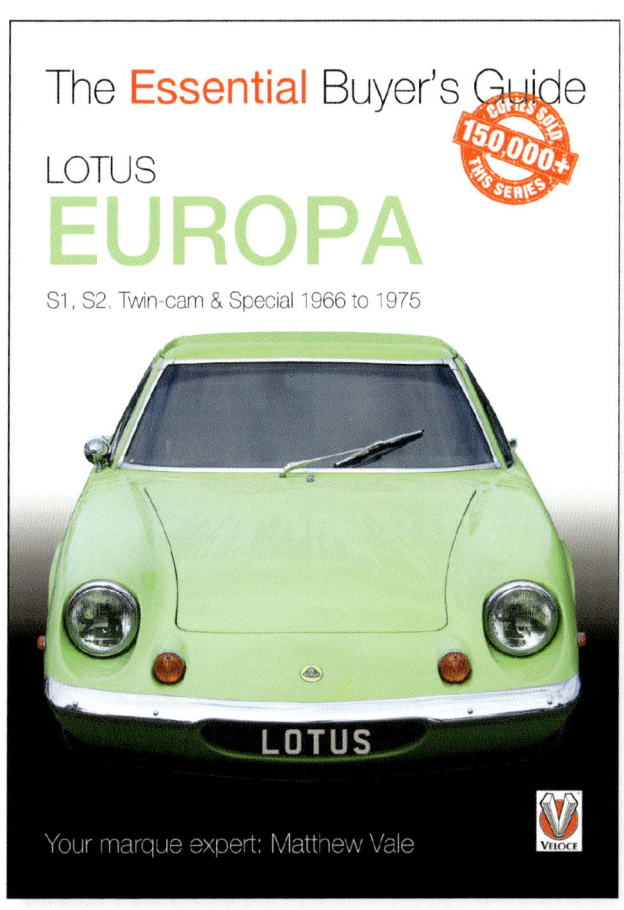

ISBN: 978-1-787112-87-2
Paperback • 19.5x13.9cm • 64 pages • 90 pictures

Interested in buying a Lotus Europa? This book will give you the background information and technical details needed to ensure you purchase the car you want. Written by an author with experience of restoring classic Lotuses.

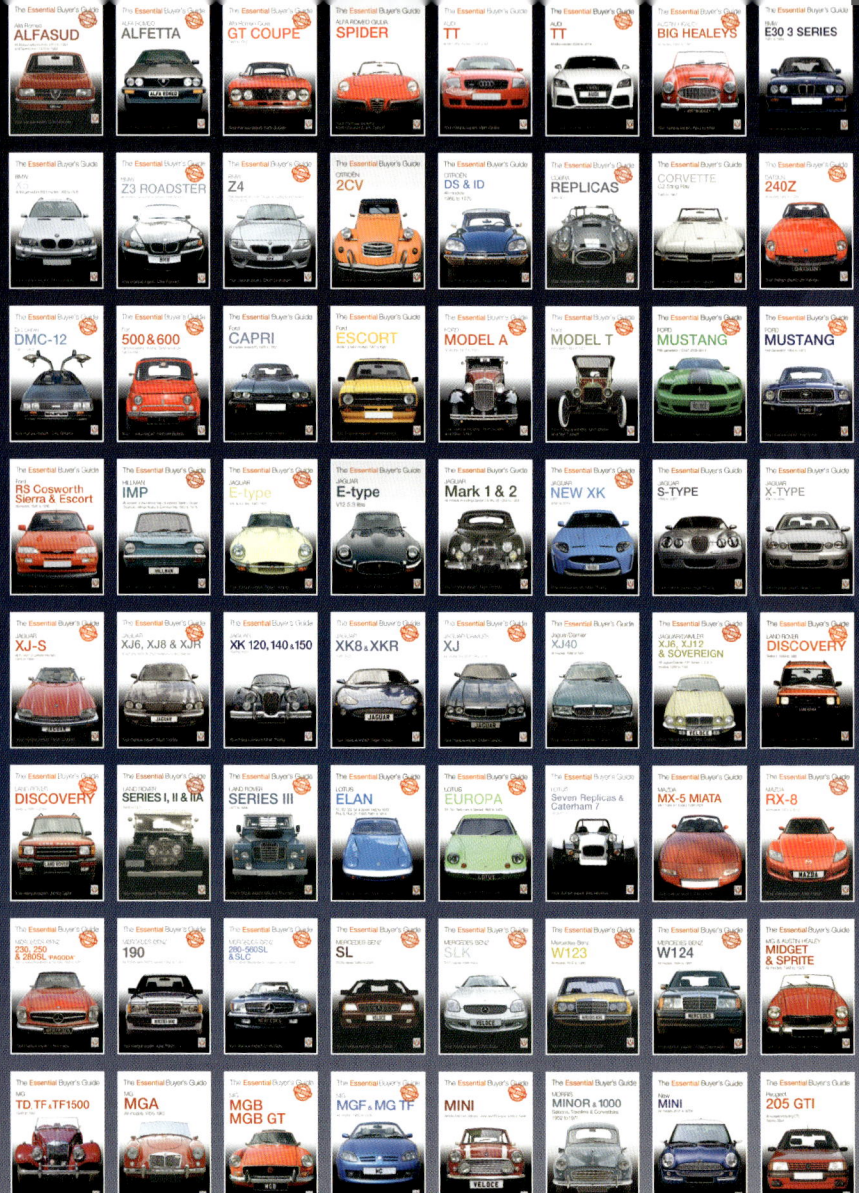

Index

Acrylic 54
Alfa Romeo Spider 9
Auctions 22, 45-46

Badges 18-19, 33
Barn find 51
Blistering 25, 53
Bodyshell 3-4, 8-9, 11-13, 16-17, 21, 23, 25-32, 50, 52, 54, 56
Bonnet 13, 18-19, 24-26, 31, 37-38
Books 56-57
Boot 6-7, 13, 15-19, 25, 31, 37, 50
Brakes – front 10, 12, 34-35, 44
Brakes – rear 10, 12, 36, 44
Bumpers 18, 26, 33

Cam cover 8, 10, 18, 26-27, 38
Cellulose 54
Certificate of provenance 21, 24, 48
Chassis 3-4, 8, 11-13, 15, 21, 23-24, 27-29, 31-32, 34-37, 41, 44, 49-50, 52, 59
Clubs 13, 48, 56
Clutch 10, 39, 41, 43, 55
Compression tester 23, 38
Cylinder head 52, 58

Dampers 27, 34, 36, 49, 52, 55
Dashboard 6, 12, 15, 19, 40-41, 52
Dellorto carburettor 7, 10, 17-19, 26, 37-38, 42, 58
Differential 18, 28, 32, 36-37, 44
Doors 6-7, 15-16, 18-19, 25, 27, 29-31, 33, 39-40, 43, 45, 52
Drain holes 31-32, 35
Driveshafts 7, 15, 18, 28, 36-37, 44, 49

Electrics 28, 40-43, 52, 55

Engine (Twin-Cam) 3-4, 6, 10, 12, 18-19, 24, 26-27, 28, 38-39, 42, 49, 50-52, 57-58
Extras 49

Fiat Dino 9
Fire 28, 42, 49

Gearbox 4, 13-14, 16, 19, 28, 39, 44, 48, 52
Gel coat 27, 29-30, 53-54
Glass fibre 3, 8-9, 12, 23, 28-29, 31, 33, 35, 39

Headlights 12-13, 41
History 20, 22, 47-48, 50
Home maintenance 7, 10
Hood – see Bonnet

Imports 47-48
Instruments 6-7, 15, 17-19, 25, 40, 43, 52
Interior 4, 6-7, 12-13, 15-19, 21, 25, 40-41, 52

Jack and jacking 23, 29, 31, 34, 36, 45
Jaguar E-Type 9, 17

Lights 11, 13, 15-17, 19, 25, 32-33, 40-41
Lotus Elite 3, 19, 57
Lotus Europa 8-9, 54, 57
Lotus Seven 8

Marcos 8
Mazda MX5 9
MG B 9
MG Midget 9
Micro-blistering 25, 30, 53-54
Minus points 8
Models – Elan 14-16
Modifications 17, 21, 49, 56
MoT test 22, 47- 48, 51

Originality 21, 24, 49

Paintwork 18, 21, 27, 29, 42, 53

Paperwork 24
Parts prices 10-11
Plus points 8
Price comparisons 14

Reliant 8
Restoration 44, 48, 51-52, 57
Rivals 9
Rotoflex donuts 7, 28, 37, 44, 49

Shock absorbers 11, 35, 55
Sills 11, 27, 31
Soft top (and hood) 4, 6, 12-13, 15-17, 25, 39, 50
Specifications 56
Steering rack 34-35
Stethoscope 23, 38
Stromberg carburettor 17, 18-19, 26, 37-38, 42, 58
Sunroof 25
Suppliers 56

Test drive 42-43, 45
Triumph GT6 9
Triumph Spitfire 9, 34
Triumph TR4 6, 9
Triumph Vitesse 34
Trunk – see Boot
TVR 8-9
Tyres 4, 12, 15, 17, 25, 33-34, 49, 52, 55, 58

Unleaded fuel 22

VIN 21, 23-24, 48, 59

Water pump 8, 10, 27-28, 52
Web resources 56
Weber carburettor 17-19, 22, 26, 37-39, 42, 58
Wheels 16-19, 23, 25-27, 29, 33-34, 42, 45, 49, 52, 58
Wishbones – front 27, 34-35
Wishbones – rear 29, 36

... don't buy a vehicle until you've read one of these!

For more details visit www.veloce.co.uk
or email info@veloce.co.uk